*Political Institutions
and Military Change*

A volume in the series

CORNELL STUDIES IN SECURITY AFFAIRS

*edited by*

Robert J. Art, Robert Jervis, *and* Stephen M. Walt

A complete list of titles in the series appears at the end of this book.

# Political Institutions and Military Change

## LESSONS FROM PERIPHERAL WARS

### Deborah D. Avant

*Cornell University Press*

ITHACA AND LONDON

First published 1994 by Cornell University Press.


Printed in the United States of America

∞ The paper in this book meets the minimum requirements
of the American National Standard for Information Sciences—
Permanence of Paper for Printed Library Materials, ANSI Z39.48-1984.

**Library of Congress Cataloging-in-Publication Data**

Avant, Deborah D. (Deborah Denise), 1958–
Political institutions and military change : lessons from peripheral wars / Deborah
D. Avant.
p.    cm. — (Cornell studies in security affairs)
Includes bibliographical references and index.
ISBN 0-8014-3034-8 (alk. paper)
1. Civil-military relations.   2. Military policy.   3. National
security.   4. Vietnamese Conflict, 1961–1975.   5. South African War,
1899–1902.   6. Malaya—History—Malayan Emergency, 1948–1960.
I. Title.   II. Series.
JF195.C5A93  1994
322'.5'0973—dc20                                                      94-16675

*To Tim, Danny, and Brandon*

# Contents

# Acknowledgments

In writing this book, I have acquired mountains of intellectual debt. I owe my interest in political science to David Laitin and Samuel Popkin. In the process of helping me write an undergraduate paper, they demonstrated an enthusiasm and an intellectual curiosity that awakened my appreciation of political science and shaped my basic perspective on the field. Working with them later only intensified my original impressions. Peter Cowhey helped me turn a general perspective into a research project and has been a model mentor: he read every draft of every chapter and has been a constant source of encouragement and ideas. (He has probably read enough drafts of each chapter to refuse a copy of the book!) Also at the University of California, San Diego, Miles Kahler, John Ruggie, Phil Roeder, and Takeo Hoshi are to be thanked—indeed, the whole political science department provided a supportive and stimulating place to learn. The Institute on Global Conflict and Cooperation (IGCC) at the University of California and the Center for International Studies (CIS) at the University of Southern California provided both financial and intellectual support for portions of this research project. In addition, I thank Michael Barnett, David Bartlett, Gary Cox, Mike Desch, Neil Englehart, Peter Feaver, Paul Kowert, Jeff Legro, Victor Magagna, Greg Nowell, John Odell, Lisa Reynolds, Andy Rutten, Brian Sala, Richard Smoke, and Stephen Van Evera for their comments on parts of the book. Part of the argument presented here appeared previously in *International Studies Quarterly* 37, no. 4 (1993).

I owe special thanks to Hendrik Spruyt and Anne Hildreth. Informal conversations with Hendrik at UCSD were invaluable for working out my argument. He remains a close personal and intellectual friend even though our offices are now three hours apart. Anne has been a source of both intellectual and emotional support since I moved to Albany. I also thank the reviewers and editors at Cornell University Press. They forced me to tighten my argument, beef up my cases, and broaden my audience. Bob Art, in particular, was a tough critic, and the book is better for it. Sam Popkin and Peter Cowhey helped me use the criticisms wisely.

My family has taken less and given more, in the time it has taken me to finish this project, than anyone should expect. My parents, Bobby and Deanna Avant, have delighted in my successes, distracted me from my failures, and paid a lot in air fare to do it. My father-in-law, Roland Herbst, read and commented on the manuscript, and has been a continual source of provocative ideas. (My mother-in-law, Gloria Herbst, sat through our conversations.) Danny and Brandon have cheerfully adjusted to whatever my schedule demanded, provided (more or less) welcome comic relief, and consistently reminded me that my job as their mom was far more important than a book "without pictures" on a subject that "most people could not even write a sentence about." I thank my husband, Tim Herbst, last because I cannot think of words that do justice to his contribution. He is my strongest advocate, my most stringent critic, my firmest base of support, and my best friend.

DEBORAH D. AVANT

*Albany, New York*

# Acronyms

ARVN   Army of the Republic of Vietnam
CAP     Combined Action Platoon
CID      Committee of Imperial Defense
CIDG   Civilian Irregular Defense Group
CIG      Central Intelligence Group
CIGS    Chief of the Imperial General Staff
CORDS Civilian Operations and Revolutionary Development Support
DDP     Directorate of Plans
DIA      Defense Intelligence Agency
DWEC  District War Executive Council
GOM   Government of Malaya
GVN    Government of Vietnam
JCS      Joint Chiefs of Staff
MAAG  Military Assistance Advisory Group
MACV  Military Assistance Command, Vietnam
MCP    Malayan Communist Party
MP       Member of Parliament
NSAM   National Security Action Memorandum
NSC     National Security Council
NVA     North Vietnamese Army
OB       Order of Battle
OCO    Office of Civilian Operations
OPC     Office of Policy Coordination
OSO     Office of Special Operations
OSS     Office of Strategic Services
SEATO  Southeast Asia Treaty Organization
SWEC   State War Executive Council
VC       Vietcong

[xi]

*Political Institutions
and Military Change*

# [1]

## The Structure of Delegation
## and Military Doctrine

Even powerful states can face disaster if their military organizations do not respond appropriately to the challenges required by the country's security strategy. The U.S. Army in Vietnam is a dramatic example of this problem. The German Army before Word War I and the French Army before World War II are also noteworthy illustrations. Why do some militaries generate doctrine that is an appropriate tool for reaching national security goals, while others do not? This question, central to studies of national security, is the focus of this book.

By examining how two countries, the United States and Britain, responded to small threats in Vietnam, South Africa, and Malaya, the book accomplishes three objectives. First, it demonstrates flaws in the conventional wisdom about the sources of military doctrine. Second, it constructs an institutional model with which we can modify the conventional wisdom to explain when military organizations will respond appropriately to a state's security goals and when they will not. Third, it tests this institutional model against other prominent explanations of military doctrine in these cases.

Theorists concerned with military doctrine and security policy have been mired in a debate about the relative significance of international and domestic variables for the formulation of defense policy. This debate has pitted international theories, which hold that military organizations should balance (or create appropriate doctrine) in response to external threats,[1] against domestic theories,

---

[1] Morgenthau (1978), Waltz (1979).

which maintain that defense policy-making is affected (usually for the worse) by organizational politics, bureaucratic rivalry, and the like.[2]

Central to this debate have been an acknowledgment that both domestic and international forces are important and periodic pleas for a model that can accurately and parsimoniously outline the interaction between domestic and international variables.[3] Institutional theory can help us construct such a model. Institutional theory provides a short cut to understanding how international and domestic variables interact and also how the interactions vary across countries.[4]

Institutional theory assumes that actors will behave so as to ensure (or enhance) their institutional power. Thus, we should expect that military organizations will be responsive to civilian goals when military leaders believe that they will be rewarded for that responsiveness. Whether military leaders expect to be rewarded or not will depend on how civilian leaders have chosen to set up and monitor military organizations. What civilian leaders have chosen depends (in democracies) on their electoral imperatives. At every level, the short-term strategies for retaining political power filter substantive policy aims to influence both civilian and military leaders' interpretation of international forces and their perspectives on national security.

## MILITARY DOCTRINE

Military doctrine is important because it affects the relations among states and the security of any particular state. Some doc-

---

[2] Allison (1971), Steinbruner (1974). Recently, a new wave of analysis has focused on democracy as a variable in the warlike behavior of states. Thus far, democracy has not been an important variable for the explanation of military doctrine per se.

[3] Allison (1971), Gourevitch (1978).

[4] Institutional theory encompasses a broad range of literature focusing on the interaction between structure and process; see March and Olsen (1984). One branch has been developed by microeconomic theorists to understand how institutional rules can shape collective choices in American politics: Calvert, Moran, and Weingast (1987); Fiorina (1981, 1982); Mayhew (1974); McCubbins and Schwartz (1984); Moe (1984, 1985, 1987, 1990); Riker (1980); Shepsle (1979, 1986); Weingast (1979)—and, in comparative politics, Bates (1981); Cowhey (1990); Hirshman (1970); North (1981,

[2]

trines can increase the chances of security dilemmas and thus heighten the probability of conflict.[5] This book, however, focuses on how military doctrine influences the security of a state.[6] I emphasize the relative integration of grand strategy and military doctrine as the fundamental determinant of how military doctrine influences the security of a state.[7] Other factors—for example, whether doctrine is offensive, defensive, or deterrent, whether it is innovative or stagnant—are important in proportion to the amount of sense they make for the state's security goals. For example, technological innovation in areas unimportant to a state's security could drain important economic resources that may, in the long term, undermine security;[8] or too much attention to the deployment of high technology against a sophisticated enemy may detract from a state's ability to deal with low-level threats from unsophisticated enemies. So I examine these variables as part of the larger integration between military doctrine and grand strategy.[9]

Sometimes security goals require militaries to be prepared for several different contingencies at the same time. It is rarely the case

---

1990); Olsen (1965); Popkin (1979). Another branch has examined how past choices become embedded in a logic that is greater than the formal rules, including myth, culture, and political norms; see Powell and DiMaggio (1991). This is not antithetical to microeconomic analyses, especially those that examine path dependency. My analysis is based on microeconomic theorizing but includes a strong element of path dependency in my analysis of how the historical growth of institutions affects the strategic expectations of individual players.

[5] See, e.g., Alexandroff and Rosecrance (1977), Jervis (1978).

[6] Posen (1984) shares this focus.

[7] Most agree that doctrine falls between the technical details of tactics and the broad outline of grand strategy. For the purposes of this book, I define tactics as issues about how battles are fought. Doctrine encompasses the broader set of issues about how one wages war. Thus, doctrine includes ideas about how best to fight an enemy and thus incorporates assumptions about what comprises the enemy. These issues have implications for tactics but do not deal with them specifically. Finally, grand strategy (or national security policy) deals with the largest set of issues. It is a theory about how to generate security for a country and therefore includes issues about which enemies a country should fight. Again, grand strategy holds implications for both doctrine and tactics. Ideally, the three should be integrated as a political means–ends chain by which a country causes security for itself. See Alger (1985), p. 7; Earle (1971), p. viii; Posen (1984), p. 13. My definitions only moderately refine those that Posen advances. See Posen, p. 245, n. 3.

[8] Kennedy (1987).

[9] Security goals include conflicts a country should avoid as well as those it should be prepared to win, so a state's grand strategy should include concerns about avoiding security dilemmas (Jervis 1978).

that a country faces only one security threat. If the threats are similar, being prepared may simply require enough troops or a good enough transportation system to meet an invasion from different sides of a country—the classic German dilemma. Sometimes, however, preparing to meet different threats actually means preparing to fight different types of war. For example, the containment doctrine required the United States to be prepared to fight communism in any guise, from the major power threat of the Soviet Union, to communist-supported uprisings in the Third World.

The cases I consider here focus on instances in which policymakers' security goals required their militaries to be prepared to meet many types of threats. The dependent variable is the integration of military doctrine with national security goals. The most important part of the dependent variable for these cases is the ability of the militaries in question to adjust doctrine to "low-tech" threats when policymakers required such adjustment to carry out their security goals.

## THE DEBATE

Organizational theory has been one of the prominent contenders in the debate between international and domestic explanations of military doctrine.[10] According to organizational theory, members of military organizations are likely to be concerned with the resources and prestige of their organization and to be mired in standard operating procedures. These conditions often prevent military organizations from responding adequately to their country's security goals. Military organizations, however, are not always unresponsive to the security needs of a country. Indeed, military doctrine is often well suited to national security goals. So organizational theory, as it has been used in the international relations literature thus far, is not sufficient to enable us to figure out the conditions under which military organizations will produce doctrine that is a good match for national security goals.[11]

---

[10] Allison (1971), Posen (1984), Snyder (1984), Steinbruner (1974).

[11] For a critique of organizational explanations of international outcomes, see Krasner (1972).

A rival explanation of military doctrine has come from balance-of-power theory. In its most general form, balance-of-power theory simply posits that states will balance one another in the international system. But as it is used to explain military doctrine, this viewpoint frequently assumes that the civilian leadership (generally the president or prime minister) will pay attention to the security interests of the country in the international system and induce changes in military doctrine when that is necessary.[12] In fact, in an innovative analysis of the sources of military doctrine before World War II, Barry Posen argues that this is precisely what happens. Although organizational theory is right about how organizations generally perform in peacetime, when a threat arises civilian leaders will intervene to force a rational updating of military doctrine in accordance with the demands of national security goals.[13]

Just as organizational theory always leads one to expect failure, however, balance-of-power theory always carries expectations of success. Neither is a good tool for understanding the variation in outcomes we see in the real world. We can, however, turn Posen's model into a theory about variation. Since the key to responsive doctrine is civilian intervention, we should expect to see militaries respond effectively to security goals when civilian leaders intervene, and to be ineffective when civilian leaders are distracted with other matters. In fact, some analysts have made just this claim. Jack Snyder's analysis of the German offensive doctrine before World War I blames a lack of civilian oversight for the poor match between military doctrine and security goals.[14] The cases in this book demonstrate, however, that civilian intervention is neither a necessary nor a sufficient condition for military responsiveness. We will see the British Army respond to civilian goals without civilian intervention and the U.S. Army resist civilian goals despite intervention.

Nonetheless, Posen and Snyder were on the right track in examining the relationship between civilian leaders and military organizations. The tools of balance-of-power theory and organizational theory, however, are too blunt to capture this relationship

---

[12] Allison (1971), model I; Morgenthau (1978); Posen (1984).
[13] Posen (1984).
[14] Snyder (1984).

effectively.[15] By using the more nuanced tools of institutional theory, we can better grasp the essence of the civil-military relationship and its effects on military doctrine.

Traditional organizational theory has been challenged by the "new" economics of organization.[16] This literature is built on the idea that organizations are rational responses to collective dilemmas. Collective dilemmas are instances where individually rational decisions lead to collectively irrational outcomes. For a variety of reasons (such as unenforceable contracts or imperfect information) neither markets nor perfect democracy (where everyone gets to vote on everything) are efficient for providing some goods.[17] We therefore delegate authority to experts or centralized authorities to make these choices for us. These principal-agent relationships occur in many forms: patient-doctor, client-lawyer, citizen–elected leader, elected leader–bureaucracy, employer-employee. In each case, a principal contracts with a specialized subordinate to provide a particular good. When civilian leaders delegate authority over portions of security policy to military organizations, however, they create new political actors and the problem of agency.[18] The organizations may not do what civilian authorities want them to.

Agency problems are exacerbated by information asymmetry and agenda setting. Because the agent has more information about his or her capabilities and performance than the principal, this information asymmetry can prevent the leader from choosing the best option (adverse selection) or cause the agent to devote more effort to the *indicators* of his or her behavior that the leader monitors, rather than the behavior itself (moral hazard). The agent's ability to control the

---

[15] Evidently, Snyder realized this. His more recent book (1991) examines the domestic basis of imperial strategies.

[16] Miller and Moe (1986).

[17] Coase (1937).

[18] See Pierson (1993) for a review of literature examining, from many perspectives (including mine), how policies affect political structure.

agenda may lead to unstable or manipulable organizational choices.[19]

The issue of agency loss is similar to the set of problems that classic organizational theory sought to explain. However, this analysis takes a much more rigorous look at the strategic political reasons for delegating power and conducts a more careful examination of how the *methods* of setting incentives for bureaucrats (monitoring their behavior and punishing failures to achieve their political task) affect policy outcomes.

Examining military organizations as agents of civilian leaders leads us to expect that the way civilians set up and oversee military organizations affects the type and degree of agency problems most likely to occur. But where do civilian decisions come from? Part of the value of the new economics-of-organization literature lies in how well it fits with other developments in theories of voting and expectations about the behavior of politicians. This literature assumes that the way leaders decide to set up and monitor organizations is influenced by their *electoral* calculations.[20] Civilian politicians cannot exercise their policy preferences unless they maintain political power.[21] Thus, the civil–military relationship is a two-tiered (or more) relationship of delegation, where voters (sometimes organized in interest groups) delegate power to civilian leaders, who then delegate a portion of that power to military organizations (Moe 1990).[22]

In this way, institutional theory also challenges the assumptions of balance-of-power theory. We should not necessarily expect to see civilian leaders behave as unitary actors pursuing the best interest

---

[19] Altfeld and Miller (1984), Hammond and Miller (1985), McCubbins (1985), Miller and Moe (1985).

[20] Influenced, but not determined. Mayhew argues that elected officials have three primary goals: to be reelected, to gain power in their institution, and to make good policy. Because they cannot pursue either of the last two goals without accomplishing the first, they will try to make good policy and gain power in their institution without jeopardizing their ability to be reelected. In some cases, this may mean handing out pork-barrel benefits to individuals or powerful interests. In other cases, it may mean pursuing a particular policy agenda. As political scientists have repeatedly discovered, what it takes to be reelected is a very individual matter. See Fenno (1978).

[21] Mayhew (1974).

[22] These theories have obviously been designed to explain behavior in democracies. It might be possible to use them to explain behavior in other systems, but one would have to model the requirements for staying in power.

of their country in the international realm. We should expect them to behave as strategic political players who act first to ensure that they will stay in power.[23] Though they should also be expected to pursue substantive goals, these goals will be conditioned by what they believe is necessary to remain in power.[24] Traditional analysts of foreign policy have contrasted theories of public interest (represented by the president responding to the international system) to theories of interest group politics or bureaucratic dominance. In contrast, this line of theorizing emphasizes how political incentives change our notions of the national interest, condition its implementation through special interest politics, and manage the ground rules for bureaucratic politics.[25] Some have followed this logic to look at how politicians (generally, members of Congress) control the bureaucracy, even when it looks as if they do not.[26] Others have examined how inefficient public policy outputs may be the result of a bureaucracy set up to ensure its superiors' maintenance of power, rather than good policy outcomes.[27]

We can also examine how the strategic interaction between politicians and bureaucracies often forces the latter to become political entrepreneurs.[28] Agents are expected to manage their arena to meet the political needs of those who control government. How an organization influences outcomes is often conditioned by the original rules and the methods by which politicians decide to oversee the

[23] Snyder's (1991) study of the development of empires creates a domestic model of civilian decisions based on a similar logic.

[24] There are moral-hazard risks on both dimensions. Politicians have a tendency to pay attention to what their constituency monitors, rather than the "national good," and military organizations may direct their behavior to the indicators that civilians monitor, rather than to the "best" military policy.

[25] Many critics of this approach have argued that it is wrong, because politicians do not always choose to make pork-barrel payoffs to constituents (Mayer 1991, Wilson 1989). But some electoral systems reward collective efforts. In Britain, where members of Parliament are nominated by party elites, politicians have an incentive to focus on collective goods (see Lijphart 1984). This approach does not specify that electoral choices must be pork barrel. Instead, it attempts to define the range of choices likely to be beneficial (or at least not harmful) to electoral success and assumes that most decisions are likely to fall within this range.

[26] McCubbins and Schwartz (1984), Weingast and Moran (1983). Others have disputed the ability of politicians to control bureaucracies (Wood 1988).

[27] Knott and Miller (1987).

[28] Altfeld and Miller (1984), Cook (1989), Hammond and Miller (1985), Miller (1992), Moe (1987, 1990).

[8]

organizations.[29] A method of oversight designed for one purpose, however, may inadvertently set up a dynamic that makes it more difficult to control the organization later.

Members of the organization acquire expectations, based on previous experience, about how political actors will behave. These expectations affect the way members of the organization will interpret new actions.[30] For example, if members of Congress routinely cast votes that benefit their districts even when their general policy proclamations are different, military leaders will pay attention to the electoral constraints under which members of Congress operate, rather than the stated policy preferences of those members. Following this line of analysis, this book investigates how institutionally conditioned civilian choices as to the setting up and monitoring of military organizations affect the strategic relationship between civilians and military organizations over time.

## AN INSTITUTIONAL MODEL OF CIVIL-MILITARY RELATIONS

A focus on the development of domestic political institutions does not ignore the effects of the international system. In this account, however, the international system is not automatically manifested in the preferences of civilian leaders. International concerns are important, but their significance for military doctrine comes through their effect on domestic political institutions.[31] International events present opportunities for domestic actors. There are always, however, a range of possible responses. Where an actor sits on this spectrum is likely to be determined by which response most benefits his or her political interests. A domestic political actor is likely to promote institutional change in response to a changing position in the international system if the shift will augment that actor's domestic political advantage.[32]

---

[29] McCubbins (1985).

[30] Miller (1992), North (1990), Popkin (1991).

[31] This is a variant of the argument made by Peter Gourevitch (1978). Gourevitch speaks of the effect of international events on both institutional structures and social forces, but his emphasis is on social forces. My argument focuses on the institutional structure. Recent studies share this focus for other issue areas. See, e.g., Haggard (1988).

[32] For a similar argument, see Rogowski (1987).

Because these parochial interests affect the way individuals in different organizations perceive the interests of the state, two different organizations may interpret the international system differently.[33] The security concerns of military leaders may be different from those of civilian leaders not because military organizations are politically parochial but because both political leaders and military organizations have political interests that influence their substantive concerns. As long as civilian leaders determine national security policy, this situation is likely to lead to unintegrated military doctrine.[34]

The new institutionalists argue that there is a fundamental difference between the structure of parliamentary and executive-legislative systems. The structure of civilian institutions influences both whether civilians will agree about what to tell the military to do (if not, they may send contradictory messages) and how civilians will monitor the military to make sure it follows their directions. Civilian leaders will have more difficulty agreeing about how to design and monitor military institutions if a division of powers exists, as in the United States. If there is only one institution responsible for controlling and monitoring the military, agreement among civilian leaders is more likely, and it is easier to set up and monitor military institutions. In this type of structure, agreement on change is also easier.

The trade-off between parliamentary and presidential structures has been discussed at length by constitutional scholars.[35] Divisions in the structure of the leadership make consensus more difficult and guards against civilian indiscretion. Unified leadership encourages concerted action but guards less against civilian indiscretion. Because change can be agreed upon and implemented more quickly,

[33] This echoes Zisk's (1990) argument that military organizations are both parochial organizations and concerned policymakers.

[34] This does not assume that civilian leaders are better able to understand the demands of the international system. However, if civilian leaders make grand strategy and military leaders, with a different vision of the state's security problems, make military doctrine, the state is less likely to have doctrine that is integrated with grand strategy. If there are institutional incentives that encourage military and civilian leaders to see the international demands in the same way or institutional incentives for military leaders to adapt to the civilian vision, it is more likely that military doctrine will be integrated with grand strategy. I thank Donald Emmerson for his pointed questions, which forced me to think this point through.

[35] Durverger (1984), Grofman and Lijphart (1986), Lijphart (1984).

[10]

civilian mistakes can be more costly. This logic is based on the electoral imperative; institutional divisions are important because if civilian leaders are elected from different constituencies and for different time periods, the likelihood that they will have different electoral incentives increases. Different electoral imperatives may induce policy disagreements and distrust between politicians in different branches of the government.[36]

Because the way civilians design military organizations is influenced by strategic political considerations, once politicians within divided institutions do agree on a solution, they may embed the agreement in the structure of an organization. In this way, they can get around constant new agreements about both what policy should be and how to control the agency. This structure, however, makes change more difficult.

Also, to the extent that the political future looks uncertain, politicians may attempt to fashion an organization in such a way as to shield it from the future authority of their political opponents.[37] This choice may make future direction of the organization more difficult. At other times, politicians may intentionally tie their own hands, to shield themselves from the political flack of an unpopular policy choice, again complicating future direction.

As the recent writings of constitutional scholars suggest, however, there are many levels of electoral rules. Some may encourage more cooperation among divided institutions. Others may encourage less cooperation among unified institutions.[38] The political context is important for determining how electoral rules and constitutional structures create electoral incentives for particular politicians.

A powerful force shaping policies for the control of the profes-

---

[36] See Huntington (1957), Mayhew (1974), Moe (1987). This argument is grounded in the literature on parliamentary versus presidential systems (Grofman and Lijphart 1986). Other studies of bureaucracy have also noticed the importance of this variable (Wilson 1989, chap. 16), as have sociologists' investigations of institutional theory. Many factors can moderate the general arrangement. Strong party control of two branches of government can lead to greater cooperation. A unified structure can be challenged with factions. (Roeder [1993] examines the differences in the level of unity within the politburo in the Soviet Union and its effect on civilian control of the military.) Overall, however, institutional divisions exacerbate coordination problems, while institutional unity mediates these problems.

[37] Moe (1990).

[38] Hammond and Miller (1985), Linz and Valenzuela (1992), Shugart and Carey (1992), Taagepera and Shugart (1989).

sional military is the original selection of personnel and incentive systems. Civilian leaders must decide how professional the military should be and how easily political leaders can intervene in the promotions process. Civilian choices about how to organize this system affect the integrity and institutional bias of the military organization.[39] An organization's *integrity* is similar to what we often call "professionalism."[40] It is the degree to which the organization presents a unified front. Standards for training, promotion, and the like induce a commonality among members of the organizations that allows us to talk about the organization's "preferences." The higher the degree of organizational integrity, the greater the ability of the organization to articulate preferences and pursue them as an actor in the political arena.[41] An organization's *institutional bias* refers to the substance of the organization's preferences. The preferences of a military organization's leadership are strongly conditioned by past civilian choices.[42] The results of these past choices are incentives embedded in the forces that promote integrity (standards for training, promotion, budgets, etc.) that condition what military leaders expect to be rewarded for. These incentives create an institutional bias that determines the organization's standard set of responses.[43]

The design of organizational incentives for professional militaries constitutes a long-term form of civilian oversight and intervention that escapes many analysts. For example, Posen's model of civil-military relations, although it drew on traditional organizational analysis, did note that civilian intervention could change bureaucratic behavior. However, because he focused only on short-term civilian influence, he did not notice the importance of long-term

[39] Civilian choices may include giving discretion to the organization to structure itself subject to broad guidelines. Civilian choice does not necessarily mean active civilian control.

[40] Huntington (1957).

[41] Miller (1992) and Kreps (1990) also argue that professionalism has a significant effect on the behavior of the agent. This argument is bolstered by Brehm and Gates (1993).

[42] Civilian choices can either be to push a military organization in a particular direction or to leave areas of military policy to the organization's discretion subject to broad guidelines (budgetary or otherwise).

[43] This is similar to Rosen's (1988) statement that each military organization has its own culture and distinct way of thinking about war that is embedded in career paths for military officers.

patterns of civilian authority for determining an organization's automatic response to a new situation (whether civilians need to intervene) and its reaction to civilian direction (whether civilian intervention will be successful).

Just because civilian leaders are not actively making military policy does not mean they are not in control. Actual civilian intervention may manifest itself only periodically. When military leaders expect that civilian leaders will use particular controls (often because they have used them before), the former will frequently act to anticipate civilian concerns, responding to them without civilian intervention. Thus, the absence of civilian intervention does not necessarily imply that there is no civilian control; it may mean that civilian leaders are satisfied.[44] How civilians are likely to intervene, as well as civilian preferences, will affect the issues to which the military will pay attention.

Furthermore, the structure of civilian institutions affects the type of short-term civilian control Posen examined. Divided civilian institutions not only enhance the possibilities for policy disagreements; they may also encourage distrust between different branches of government over the control of bureaucracy. Once this distrust develops, it can limit the way politicians choose to use personnel to control the bureaucracy. When members of Congress have checks on personnel appointments—if, for example, they can refuse to confirm presidential appointments or hold hearings to see whether the president was correct to fire military leaders—these checks cause the president to be careful about anticipating Senate preferences when appointing military leaders and to look for special circumstances before firing a military leader in the midst of a crisis.[45] When distrust is established, presidents will be more likely to use noncontroversial personnel appointments to shape the overall tenor of a military organization than to dictate change in crisis situations.[46]

[44] Formal theorists call this a *fallacy of the equilibrium*.

[45] Even when Truman had much congressional support for firing MacArthur, his foes drew political blood through hearings, and so on. Lincoln's removal of McClellan during the Civil War and Johnson's removal (or at least promotion) of Westmoreland after the Tet Offensive in Vietnam were free from political costs, because the actions endorsed congressional convictions.

[46] In other words, presidents will be unlikely to reach down into the ranks for new perspectives and will be reluctant to dictate change by firing military leaders in a crisis.

This has important ramifications for the ability of civilians to intervene during crises. Analyses of successful civilian intervention have demonstrated that promoting new innovative leaders is an effective tool for generating innovation.[47] Other control mechanisms are less likely to generate appropriate change quickly. If presidents are less likely to use personnel to direct military change in crisis situations and other control mechanisms are less likely to promote effective change, the automatic response of military institutions to new situations will be more important when civilian control is divided.[48]

I join many new analyses of military organizations in challenging the assumption that all military organizations behave similarly.[49] Most of these analyses, however, have focused on the qualities *within* the military organizations to explain variation in behavior and preferences. Kimberly Zisk has argued that military policymakers are not only bureaucratic entities trying to preserve the health of their organization but also state actors trying to pursue national security.[50] Given this, she contends, crisis intervention by civilian leaders to *force* military organizations to adopt new doctrine may not be the best avenue for military change. Instead, if civilian leaders choose less confrontational methods (e.g., widening the policy community by bringing in analysts with new ideas), they can persuade, rather than force, military leaders to change. The key to military innovation is changing the minds of military personnel. A similar approach is taken by Stephen Rosen, who looks specifically at *when* military organizations will innovate, or adapt to new threats.[51] He challenges

[47] Posen (1984), Mearsheimer (1983), Weigley (1976). Rosen (1991) argues that promoting military mavericks is not an effective way of directing military change. In predicting the potential for successful use of personnel, then, we may want to distinguish between mavericks and other policy outliers who are better able to work with the system.

[48] These strategies may include attempts to shape the way individuals in military organizations think. Much of the information traded in formal organizations is more persuasive than factual. See Bailey (1991).

[49] Kier (1992), Rosen (1988, 1991), Wilson (1989), Zisk (1990).

[50] Zisk (1990).

[51] Rosen separates military innovation into three categories: peacetime, wartime, and technological. In both peacetime and wartime categories, innovation is defined as either a change in how one of the primary combat arms of a service fights or the addition of a new arm. Technological innovation, on the other hand, may or may not affect how a service fights. New technologies may simply be used to support existing practices better. The dependent variable I am examining here is not technological

Posen's contention that military organizations innovate only in response to civilian intervention. Instead, he suggests we look at military organizations as complex political communities, each with its own culture or rules about how people should behave and interact. Innovation, he argues, requires an ideological struggle to redefine the values of the community or the strategic measures of effectiveness. Such a struggle is likely to result when senior military leaders formulate a strategy for innovation. Although civilian leaders can be supportive of the military leadership, they cannot (because they are outsiders to the community) spur innovation themselves—neither can military mavericks, who, bucking the values of the community, lack the requisite political capital to change the community's values.

Though Zisk focuses on the policy community, and Rosen on military leadership, both look for variation within the military organizations. Some analysts of principal-agent problems have made similar claims that the quality of the agent is more important than oversight by the principal.[52] My analysis differs in that it examines both the structure of civilian institutions and how civilian leaders choose to set up and oversee military organizations as the crucial variables for determining how an organization's integrity and bias will develop.[53] While not discounting the importance of the agent's bias or the military organization's culture or mind-set, I argue that bias is not created in a vacuum but is established over time through the organization's interactions with its civilian superiors in an electoral context.

In addition, although both Rosen and Zisk argue that military organizations are not all the same, they continue to assume that in general, military organizations are resistant to change, that noninnovation is more or less the natural state of an organization.[54] A principal-agent model suggests that the propensity of an organization to innovate is a property of the incentives created by the structure of delegation. In fact, some organizations have within their ethos attention to change and flexibility. In these cases, innovation

innovation but a change in the orientation of a service or service branch in response to a new or changed adversary in both peacetime and wartime. See Rosen (1992).
[52] Brehm and Gates (1990).
[53] For a review of this general way of using institutional history, see Pierson (1993).
[54] This is echoed in Wilson's (1989) analysis.

does not require an ideological struggle: the changes made by the U.S. Marines in Vietnam and the British Army during the Boer War did not require one. A change in the measure of strategic effectiveness for these organizations came fairly naturally, given their structural incentives.[55]

A more detailed perspective on military culture is offered by Elizabeth Kier (1992). She argues that civilian leaders' choices about military doctrine are mediated by the culture of a military organization. Culture provides the framework that shapes interests in a particular political-military context. Kier focuses less on the variety of domestic and international variables that influence the political military context and more on cultural situations. She outlines two types of cultural situations in the political-military context: *consensual,* in which subcultures generally agree, and *unsettled,* in which there is strong disagreement between two or more subcultures. She argues that civilian leaders are more likely to respond to the international system when a consensual cultural situation exists whereas when culture is unsettled, civilians are busy trying to fight domestic battles and are distracted from the issues in the international system.

In interesting ways, the expectations of the consensual-versus-unsettled cultural situation parallels the expectations generated by unified-versus-divided institutions. The institutional model, however, focuses more on the institutional *conditions* under which agreement is more or less likely. The institutional structure within which agreement is reached is important for generating expectations about what forces will be likely to undermine the agreement.

A central feature in Rosen's analysis is that promotion policies are the tools by which military leaders induce change in their organization. Changes in the rules of the community come through changes in the reward structure. Senior military leaders with the requisite political capital and knowledge of the organization's culture can best implement their commitment to innovation by changing the way personnel are promoted.[56]

Rosen is right to argue that promotion policies are crucial to military change. However, as institutional analysts have demonstrated

[55] See Chapters 2, 4, and 5.
[56] This issue is not disputed by Kier (1992), who rejects the dichotomy between interests and culture.

[16]

in other policy areas, promotion policies can also be used effectively by civilian leaders to induce a particular perspective among military leaders.[57] The cases in this book show how promotion policies are a function of the politics of delegation. Furthermore, other oversight mechanisms (e.g., the annual budgetary process, reauthorization of programs, watchdog agencies or groups, and important rewards and sanctions) also play a large role in the development of an organization's bias.

The significance of the institutional model is that it delineates where military bias comes from and suggests other implications for reform than do models that focus on the dynamics within organizations. Although I do not discount the (mis)perceptions that result from an organization's bias, I assume that these perceptions are tied to incentives and that as incentives change, so do perceptions. In addition, I argue that civilian choices fundamentally condition the possibilities for future organizational bias. For example, ideas were obviously important in the development of both armies' biases.[58] The U.S. Army adopted the scientific ideas of the Prussian Army, a decision that profoundly influenced the future course of the former. The British Army adopted ideas about how scientific principles had to be altered to fit the particularly British military challenge, and this had significant effects on the growth of the army in Britain. However, not all ideas have such an important effect. Despite the wealth of new ideas on counterinsurgency provided by a broadening of the policy community during the Kennedy administration, counterinsurgency did not take hold. This is explained by the lack of career incentives. No matter what the president said and no matter how many new ideas were introduced, as long as individuals who focused on counterinsurgency in the Army moved up the career ladder more slowly, the counterinsurgency "revolution" was not likely to be successful. New ideas are important, but past civilian choices affect whether or not new ideas will actually influence policy outcomes. Ideas are only as strong as the incentives that support them.

Finally, this argument points to some inherent difficulties with

---

[57] Moe (1984).

[58] See Goldstein (1989) and Odell (1982) for analyses focusing on the role of ideas. Zisk's (1990) focus on policy communities also outlines a significant role for ideas.

[17]

generating military responsiveness when actions that will achieve this end may threaten the career prospects of *civilian* leaders. Given that civilian leaders are unlikely to threaten their own careers, measures for reform should pay close attention to the political imperatives of civilian leaders.

A NOTE ON THE CASES

This book examines the U.S. Army in Vietnam and the British Army in the Boer War and Malaya to test the explanation drawn from institutional theory against the traditional wisdom. One could argue that these cases are poor tests of the dominant literature on military doctrine. The explanations relying on balance-of-power theory, in particular, often focus on major wars between big powers, where each is truly threatening to the territorial sovereignty of the other.[59] Adherents of these models might argue that the U.S. Army did not adapt in Vietnam because the Vietnamese communists never threatened U.S. security.

However, because balance-of-power theories hinge on the structural position of a state in the international system, to the degree that these models are helpful in shaping predictions about military doctrine, we should expect countries in similar international positions to generate comparable military responses to similar threats.[60] The cases (the United States in Vietnam and the British in the Boer War) were carefully selected for their similarities both in the structural positions of the major powers and the nature of the small threat.[61]

Britain was clearly regarded as the economic hegemon during the nineteenth century, and the United States assumed a similar role after World War II.[62] Additionally, for somewhat different reasons, each had articulated a grand strategy that required it to meet chal-

---

[59] Mearsheimer (1983), Posen (1984); see also Snyder (1984), Van Evera (1985).

[60] A number of analysts use this logic to explain why major powers often lose peripheral wars. See Cohen (1986), Huntington (1982), Mack (1983).

[61] The Malayan case was added to control for the nature of jungle warfare and to demonstrate continued difference between the U.S. and British Armies.

[62] I do not mean to imply that these countries assumed equal predominance. The United States was a greater "great power" than was Britain.

lenges from small powers. In the United States this prompted limited wars against communist forces in both Korea and Vietnam. In Britain, it prompted a host of small wars toward the end of the nineteenth century, culminating in the war against the Boers in South Africa. In the context of their grand strategies, both countries defined these particular wars as extremely important. Vietnam was a test case for the credibility of extended deterrence. The British were fighting for their credibility in the colonies and with other European powers.[63] Thus, if balance-of-power theory is ever useful for explaining military responses to anything less than world wars, one should expect Britain and the United States to respond in a similar fashion to these important peripheral threats.[64]

More important, the dynamics of Posen's model, which captures the general wisdom on this subject, should work in all cases. Military organizations should prefer offensive doctrine and be reluctant to change. Civilian leaders should be more attuned to the demands of the international system and should intervene to force change if the threat is significant enough. Once political leaders intervene, they should be able to force rationalizing changes in military doctrine.

The cases in this book demonstrate that we need to improve on the general wisdom in three ways. First, we need to account for variations among the standard responses of military organizations. All military organizations do not share the same biases. Second, although Posen and Snyder pointed us in the right direction by suggesting that we pay attention to civilian direction of the military,

---

[63] In 1899, the opposition (Liberal) leader Herbert Asquith said in a speech to Parliament that the struggle now went much deeper than a mere question of asserting and maintaining the British position in South Africa: "It is our title to be known as a world power which is now up on trial" (Packenham 1979, p. 258).

[64] There are "balancing" concerns in both multipolar and bipolar situations that could cause major powers to attach importance to peripheral areas. For example, U.S. action in Korea and Vietnam became part of a broader claim about the country's credibility as an alliance partner. (If the United States would not stand ground against communists in Vietnam, would it in Europe?) These may manifest themselves in a shared belief among states that elevates the importance of certain peripheral areas at particular times for specific reasons. At some level, we could imagine that a different reason for involvement in a peripheral area could affect the outcome of military doctrine. For example, does it matter that Britain was not fighting in South Africa to display its commitment to its allies, as the United States (arguably) was in Vietnam? The answer to this question may complicate, but should not contradict, my story.

[19]

their theoretical tools led them to focus on crisis intervention. In fact, there are many other long-term ways in which civilians direct the military. I argue that this direction holds the key to the variation in military bias. Finally, how civilians direct the military is conditioned not only by the international system but also by what civilians must do to maintain domestic power. Thus, civilian leaders' interpretations of analogous international circumstances differ from country to country. Institutional theory provides the necessary tools for modeling these new assumptions.

PLAN OF THE BOOK

Chapter 2 examines the development of integrity and bias in the U.S. and British Armies. I argue that electorally conditioned civilian choices led to quite different modes of professionalism in the U.S. and British Armies. Chapter 3 demonstrates how the U.S. Army's bias led it to be resistant to presidential efforts to induce a focus on counterinsurgency doctrine before and during the Vietnam War. Furthermore, it shows how congressional decisions about how to oversee military organizations unintentionally hindered presidential attempts to force the Army to change. Chapter 4 examines those U.S. military organizations that did adapt to the challenges of counterinsurgency in Vietnam. It demonstrates how politicians' decisions about how to structure and monitor these organizations induced a bias toward flexibility that enhanced the possibility that these organizations would adapt. It also, however, shows how the Army's domination of such agenda items as the criterion for success hindered these adaptive organizations from dominating U.S. doctrine in Vietnam. Chapter 5 analyzes the British experience in the Boer War and Malaya to demonstrate how the British Army's bias led it to be both more attuned to the demands of particular conflicts and (in the Malayan case) less resistant to civilian intervention. Chapter 6 draws the implications of these case studies and the logic of the new institutionalism for future research on security problems.

# [2]

# Civil-Military Relations in the United States and Britain

The patterns of professionalism and bias in the British and American armies are different. This chapter explains why. The roots of the variations lie in the way civilian leaders chose to set up and oversee the armies. Civilian choices influenced what military leaders expected to be rewarded for. Furthermore, civilian leaders chose to oversee military organizations in a way that enhanced their ability to maintain domestic power. The difference in electoral rules between the two countries, then, was an important issue in the development of different military biases.

In the United States, concern over the usurpation of power by any one person or group led the founders to set up a system of checks and balances that institutionalized divisions among the civilian leadership. Civilian institutions were induced to concern themselves with monitoring one another as well as the military. Because civilian institutions in the United States cater to different constituencies, members have different electoral concerns and thus different policy preferences. This made it hard for civilian leaders in the United States to agree on policy. Institutional divisions also induced distrust between the civilian branches of government, distrust that influenced the mechanisms civilians chose to control military organizations.

The structure was designed to produce a check on civilian institutions—as Madison argued, to induce the government leaders to control each other.[1] Because it made agreement among civilian leaders

[1] See *Federalist* No. 10.

more difficult than it would have been under an undivided system, this structure made agreeing on change more difficult. Also, once civilian leaders agreed on a solution they often embedded the agreement in the structure of the organization. In this way they avoided constant need for new agreements on how to control the bureaucracy. Once again, however, this structure made change more difficult.

Institutions developed differently in Britain. Changes in the nineteenth century centralized power over policy-making in the Cabinet. With only one institution beholden to the same constituency responsible for controlling the military, we should expect that Britain would have an easier time devising oversight procedures to ensure that military policy did not diverge from civilian preferences. In a structure that makes agreement easier, agreement on change is also easier. This system, however, is less guarded than its U.S. counterpart against civilian indiscretion. Because changes in civilian goals can be agreed upon and carried through more easily, civilian mistakes can be more costly.

Although examining the structure of civilian authorities can take us a long way toward understanding what problems people in different institutional structures will encounter with respect to security issues, explaining specific policy outcomes requires a more careful look at the historical circumstances under which the civil-military relationship develops. The political context affects both the substantive preferences and relative power of civilian leaders and military organizations. The context also affects how civilians choose to oversee military organizations. The way such oversight works at each step in the process, in turn, affects the integrity and bias of the military organization and thus the range of future military responses.

For example, there are several alternatives that would allow divided civilian leaders both to balance one another and to manage the military. Divided civilian institutions in England after the English Civil War chose to accomplish these ends by keeping the Army from developing any organizational integrity. The Army was effectively dismantled after every war; officers purchased their commissions (to ensure that only the propertied class would gain power) and were expected to be gentlemen first and officers only in time of war. In the United States, similar concerns were resolved by allowing the Army to develop a very high degree of integrity. Both strategies were reasonable guards against one civilian institution's usurping the power of another. The British Army was staffed by men from the same social class as Parliament and was absolutely weak as an organization. It would have been useless to usurpers. The U.S. Army with its strong sense of corporate identity would be less malleable to a usurper's goals.

The alternative chosen, however, had significant effects on the structure of the organizations; and the structure of the organizations influenced their preferences and abilities as political players.[2] The professional army in the United States was better able to pursue its political interests than the disorganized army in nineteenth-century Britain. Because that was the case, as the U.S. Army became professionalized, strategic leaders were able to structure the organization in such a way as to pursue their preferences.

In particular, in the U.S. case, military leaders were able to induce a focus on the deductive notions of military science (based on the Prussian experience) that were in vogue in military circles at that time. Early decisions by civilian leaders in the United States to grant autonomy over professional development to the military led to a greater influence of such deductive analyses on professionalism. In Britain, where professionalization was closely supervised by civilian leaders, those military leaders more interested in Britain's most pressing security concerns were rewarded. Military professionalism in the abstract came to include notions of adaptability—using "military science" only as it pertained to the specifics of the British position. More deductive theorists were left outside the policy process in Britain. Thus, both institutional structures and political choices contributed to the development of different biases in these two armies.

## Development of Civil-Military Institutions in the United States

As I stated earlier, the system of checks set up by the founders complicated civilian agreement on policy. Disagreements between

---

[2] Psychologists have pointed to the dynamics by which the structure of delegation might influence the preferences of actors within an organization. The structure of

Congress and the president also affected civilian choices about how to direct the military's behavior.[3] American institutions gave the greatest priority to providing Congress and the president checks and balances over each other.

### Prehegemonic Civil-Military Relations

Initially, however, Congress and the president did not compete over control of the Army. Congressional concern over national military policy before the turn of the century was distracted by its overwhelming concern with the militia. Because state parties controlled congressional nominations and received many political benefits from their control over the militia, congressmen had electoral reasons to pay attention to militia, rather than army, matters.

During the Civil War, however, when military matters did have a large impact on electoral politics, Congress became more concerned with military matters. As the Civil War began, President Lincoln appointed a general who supported his conciliatory policies toward the South. Lincoln sought merely to suppress the insurrection without allowing it to degenerate into "a violent and remorseless revolutionary struggle." True to this, General George B. McClellan (a Democrat) developed a strategy that avoided the pitched battles characteristic of the Napoleonic wars. Instead, he opted for sieges in the formal style of eighteenth-century limited wars. His principal strategic objective was not to destroy the enemy's army but to capture the Confederate capital.[4]

Congress was dissatisfied with this conciliatory doctrine. Lincoln remained committed to McClellan and his plans much longer than his party in Congress did. However, as the policy seemed to produce a stalemate, Lincoln, too, began to question McClellan's approach,

---

delegation provides the set of short-term goals that members of the organization must pay attention to in order to keep their jobs. Actors will attempt to find congruence between what they must do to keep their jobs and what is required for national security, in order to minimize cognitive dissonance. If there are significant differences between short-term goals and national security, actors may redefine the latter so that their behavior to achieve short-term goals will also achieve national security. See Akerlof (1984). See also Jervis (1976).

[3] Huntington (1957), p. 177.

[4] See Weigley (1976), pp. 44–46; see also Bernardo and Bacon (1955), pp. 214–22; Lincoln (1953–55), vol. 4.

and when McClellan did not respond, Lincoln fired him. Lincoln's replacement of McClellan with Ulysses S. Grant was so successful because Congress approved of it. When Lincoln finally decided to abandon the formal war doctrine pursued by McClellan in 1862, he was heartily endorsed by Congress; McClellan, with nowhere to turn for support, was removed from office.[5] Lincoln and Secretary of War Edward M. Stanton then maintained personal control over the Army until Grant proved himself at the battles of Vicksburg and Chattanooga. When Grant demonstrated success with a doctrine of annihilation, Congress endorsed Lincoln's selection by reviving the full rank of lieutenant general in order to give him complete control over the Union Army.[6]

Congress supported the president's leadership of the Army during the Civil War because the two institutions came to agree upon a strategy. In the period after Lincoln's assassination, however, Congress and the president were bitterly divided. Given these divisions, the military was able to support the policies of the institution that most aligned with its interests.[7] The Army and congressional Republicans both sought to restructure power in the South.[8] The Army wanted to follow through with its mission of overcoming the defeated enemy and protect its men stationed in the South, and congressional Republicans wanted to maintain their power against bids for election by former Confederates. Imposing Negro suffrage in the South through military occupation was a way to accomplish both of these goals.[9]

After the 1866 election gave the Republicans a working majority in Congress ostensibly large enough to override a presidential veto,

---

[5] Weigley (1984), pp. 245–46.

[6] See Weigley (1984), p. 249; Williams (1952), pp. 302–3.

[7] Hyman (1960).

[8] Army personnel were attacked legally (Southern courts entertained damage suits against individual soldiers), and harassed (those stationed in the South were subject to many personal risks when on leave). See Hyman (1960), pp. 85–100; Weigley (1984), p. 258. Congressional Republicans feared that the president's policies would allow delegates elected from the former Confederate States to take seats in the national legislature, and they prevented these "Confederate brigadiers" from taking seats in 1866. See Hyman (1960), Weigley (1976, 1984).

[9] I am not suggesting that the military was running politics during Reconstruction. I am merely pointing out that the differences in opinion between the president and Congress allowed the military to support the branch whose policies most closely represented their own preferences. See Thomas and Hyman (1962).

Congress set to work on Reconstruction legislation that included much of what the Army wanted—the continuation of martial law, legal protection of army personnel, and the disenfranchisement of most former rebels. Furthermore, it moved to circumvent presidential authority over Grant and Stanton through the Command of the Army Act and the Tenure of Office Act of March 1867. Johnson's attempt to evade these by replacing Stanton led to the impeachment proceedings against him.[10]

The events of the Civil War demonstrate that even in divided governments, when civilian institutions come to strong agreement on policy, presidents can effectively control military organizations in a crisis by hiring and firing military leaders. The events of Reconstruction, however, demonstrate how a president who tries to control the Army by firing military leaders can run grave risks when Congress does not agree with his policies. Perhaps more important, however, once the events of Reconstruction had happened, both presidents and Army leaders paid attention to the risks of presidential meddling in military affairs.

After the Civil War, the Army became professionalized in a state of isolation. Congress was content to let the Army set its own standards for education, training, promotion, evaluations, and retirement relatively free from interference so long as it did not request an increased budget. Presidents, free from any pressing external threat and well aware of the costs of meddling, left the Army to develop its professional standards free from civilian influence.[11]

The resulting bias was influenced by the regard with which the Army held the military progress of the Prussians.[12] The American Army developed a highly deductive method for understanding and preparing for wars, relying heavily on the Prussian "science of war." The Army objected to the use of the armed forces as a police force (because it was beneath the soldier's vocation) and argued that the Army must always be governed by classic military principles. It developed preferences that were characteristically biased toward offen-

---

[10] Hyman (1960), pp. 96–97; Weigley (1984), p. 260; White (1958), pp. 22–23. The "Command of the Army Act" was actually a provision attached to the Army Appropriations Act. See Weigley (1984), p. 646, n. 47; *Statutes at Large* 14 (1867): 486–87.

[11] Huntington (1957); Weigley (1984), pp. 272–92.

[12] Alger (1982), Ambrose (1964), Reardon (1990), Upton (1972).

sive, decisive doctrine—generally, doctrine based on the European experience and appropriate for the European theater.[13]

The impact of the Army's mode of preparing for war is most clearly illustrated by the idea of "safe leadership." Through the efforts of such prominent military theorists of the late nineteenth century as William Sherman and Emory Upton, the Army institutionalized a system of education for its officers. The key to this educational system was a focus on military history to teach the principles of war and cultivate uniformity of thought and procedure. Through uniform application of these principles, the Army would ensure that the individual qualities of leaders would be relatively unimportant, that officers educated in these institutions would respond the right way to military uncertainties and thus be "safe" leaders.[14]

As Carol Reardon (1990) has pointed out, the inculcation of standards of professionalism was common to many different entities in the United States at the time. Professionalizing reforms also swept across organizations in many other countries at the turn of the century. However, despite the efforts of a number of skilled researchers and teachers who fought to teach military principles in a contextual framework and to apply the principles to the particular problems faced by the American military, the principles of war taught in the Army's educational institutions led more and more to a rigid understanding of warfare.

This was in part due to War Department inaction. The War Department took a low profile role in the development of military history in the United States. Unlike the British Parliament, the civilians leaders in the United States refused to issue official support for military histories focusing on the particularly American problems of defense.[15] So while military books emanated from Europe with the official sanction of the general staff of the country of provenance,

---

[13] Of course, whether offensive doctrine is appropriate even in this theater is subject to debate (Miller 1985).

[14] See Reardon (1990), pp. 35–49.

[15] In 1895 the adjutant general issued a policy that warned of the problems of official sanctions on behalf of American authors when so many military men seemed content to buy and read the better-known European authors (ibid., pp. 100–101).

in the United States military authors had to go it alone.[16] With no official civilian guidance, advocates of different approaches to preparation for warfare in the United States fought it out among themselves, and—unsurprisingly—the more traditional supporters of the classic European principles won.[17]

The focus on Germany per se is not what is most interesting for the comparison with Britain. After all, it has been argued that the United States did "Americanize" the Prussian lessons. The important thing is the deductive method that relies on a particular, or "appropriate," reading of history. In the American Army—as in the Prussian Army—the science of war triumphed over the art of war. Deductive principles and rigid training overcame the importance of context and the art of understanding a particular conflict.[18]

The strong support for the science of war led the idea of safe leadership to take on a strong bias against individual initiative. Safe leadership came to mean that officers could make their careers safe from risky uncertainties by following the letter of the Army regulations. By rewarding leaders who adhered to regulations, rather than those who used their judgment, the American Army developed an institutional bias toward timeless principles, rather than particular applications.

During the late nineteenth century, when the U.S. Army became professionalized, congressional oversight of Regular Army training activities was largely (almost completely) based on finance.[19] Military leaders learned that budgetary requests would prompt congressional scrutiny and acted to shape the development of the military institution without increased budgetary requests.[20] Although orga-

---

[16] This was not only a status problem but a financial one; with no War Department sanction, there was also no War Department funding (ibid.).

[17] In 1908 the first military history textbook was adopted by the U.S. Army's postgraduate schools. Written by Captain Matthew Forney Steele, *American Campaigns* was the standard textbook in army classrooms up through World War II. Though written about the American experience, the book used American history to illustrate predetermined principles of warfare and "helped perpetuate the deductive applicatory methods of teaching the art of war." Reardon (1990), p. 109.

[18] Reardon (1990), pp. 109–44.

[19] Skowronek (1982), pp. 90–97; see also Thain (1901).

[20] Huntington (1957), pp. 226–36; Weigley (1984), p. 283. An alternative explanation could be that Congress liked what the Army was doing. I have no evidence to refute this claim aside from the fact that Congress paid little attention to (and thus seemed to have little information about) the Army's internal organization.

nizational theorists would argue that the Army should be naturally hungry for more budgetary resources, Army leaders acted strategically. They both valued autonomy and understood that the chances of significant budgetary increases from Congress were slight. They therefore formulated proposals for reforms that would not require budgetary increases, to ensure that their programs would not be too closely scrutinized (and then politicized) by Congress. Congress was regarded with suspicion by the rising military professionals.

> So long as the Army was kept down to twenty-five thousand men, Congress let the West Pointers run it in accordance with their own ideas. So long as the number of officers was kept low, Congress approved changes in promotion and retirement plans. Sherman, for instance, carefully avoided Congress in setting up the School of Application at Leavenworth; he did not wish it to be "the subject of legislation." Subsequently, he repeatedly pointed out that the schools at both Leavenworth and Monroe required no additional funds beyond "ordinary garrison expenses." And Congress, content with this, shrugged its shoulders and let them be.[21]

### Hegemonic Civil-Military Relations

Two significant and interrelated changes altered congressional interest in military affairs at the turn of the century. First, the rising power of the United States in the international system made military power more salient to American politics. Simultaneously, the progressive reforms loosened the ties between congressional nominations and state parties and opened the way for a more nationally oriented Congress.[22] In response to these changes, Congress reorganized its oversight of the military. As military power became more important to American politics and national politics became more important than local politics for congressional careers, Congress became more interested in military activity.

[21] Huntington (1957), p. 234. He points out that five of the six other advanced schools established by the Army between 1865 and 1914 were first set up by departmental order without prior congressional authorization. Because they required no additional funds, Congress did not have to approve expenditures.
[22] See Galloway (1976), Kernell (1977), McCormick (1986), Price (1971), Skowronek (1982).

Congress's enhanced role in military affairs, which was formally institutionalized after World War II, *increased* the Army's ability to resist presidential direction. Army leaders used congressional interest in military affairs to insulate themselves from presidents' attempts at intervention. By protecting the military from undue intervention by the president, increased congressional interest in military matters did not allow easier civilian direction over military doctrine but intensified the Army's resistance to change.

The prominent role the United States had played in World War II, along with the dissolution of the allies after Germany's defeat, generated the opportunity for the United States to play a much larger international role than it had in the past. And given that, members of Congress also had incentives to enhance the part the legislature played in the management of defense and to boost their individual roles in bringing home the local benefits of the new national policy.

Congress's more active role in military policy generated two trends. First, national security policy began to reflect shorter-term, parochial concerns. This was simply a function of the different electoral demands on Congress and the president, resulting in two different views of the international system. Presidents are often more interested in the security demands of the international system, because *national* security is closely tied to their electoral security. Members of Congress are more likely to be influenced by concerted interests in their constituency, which favors a *local* reading of the international system.[23] Members of Congress also have a greater opportunity to blame others for national security failures.[24] It is harder for Congress to share both the credit and the blame for national security policy.[25] Therefore, members of Congress have less incentive to heed the "objective" demands of the international system, especially if it will cause them electoral harm. When the National Security Act of 1949 enhanced Congress's input into national security policy, it simultaneously increased the chances that a par-

[23] For example, members with naval yards in their district will be more likely to see national security goals that require a bigger or better navy.

[24] This strategy is generally less successful for members of Congress who are of the president's party.

[25] Blechman (1990), pp. 5–6.

ticular military doctrine would become entrenched in local political goals.[26]

An active congressional role in the formation of national security policy also complicated presidential attempts to direct biased military agents, by increasing the political risks of hiring and firing military leaders. In the most dramatic example of this, President Truman's experience with General Douglas MacArthur in the Korean War demonstrated to future presidents that firing a military commander during a war was a politically risky way to direct military doctrine. Despite the fact that President Truman enjoyed broad support in Congress for his removal of MacArthur, a small minority of congressional foes used the event to hold hearings and publicly embarrass the president. This resulted in a tendency for presidents to reach toward micromanagement, rather than dramatic personnel changes, to reorient military organizations.[27] Micromanagement attempts, however, were subject to moral-hazard problems. Because Army leaders had more information than the president, the Army was often able to skirt presidential direction or alter its impact.

Presidents have been more successful directing military organizations with ordinary appointments. By selecting officers who agree with presidential goals, they can affect the future leadership priorities. This, however, requires high-level officers who agree with presidential goals. In the event that high-level officers have relatively uniform preferences, the president may have to reach down into the ranks to promote change (as we shall see with the Army in Vietnam). However, if the president has to reach down into the ranks, the appointment process becomes less ordinary and more politically risky.

---

[26] This parochial focus does not simply create a barrel of pork out of military policy. For an argument that serious national goals influence even what is typically regarded as the biggest pork barrel—weapons procurement—see Mayer (1991). When policy recommendations are uncertain (as they generally are), however, members of Congress will be more likely to choose policies—rationalized on the basis of national security—that favor (or at least do not hurt) their electoral futures. This has certainly made the formation of defense policy a more political game.

[27] Weigley (1976) argues that the success of Lincoln's control over military doctrine in the Civil War was due to his choices in personnel—McClellan (committed to a conciliatory strategy) in the first part of the war and Grant (committed to a total-war strategy) for the second. Of course, Huntington (1957) points out that the control over personnel runs greater risks of degenerating into "subjective civilian control," or the politicization of the military.

[31]

Congress continued to rely on budgetary policy to direct the military. After World War I, however, Congress had changed budgetary procedures in a way that resulted in interservice rivalry.[28] The change was intended to enhance congressional oversight. The policy change, combined with questions about new technology (air power), led to increased competition among the service branches. The competition among the branches presented Congress with competing strategic visions: it could fund the vision it preferred.[29]

In its efforts to restructure the defense policy-making machinery after World War II so as to enhance its members' role in defense policy-making, Congress continued to rely on interservice rivalry.[30] The National Security Act of 1947 and 1949 reflect this concern. In particular, Congress ensured that the president would take advice from policy experts and also that Congress would have access to military advice.[31] The 1949 act permitted a member of the Joint Chiefs of Staff (JCS) to present to Congress, "on his own initiative, after first informing the Secretary of Defense, any recommendation relating to the Department of Defense that he may deem proper."[32]

In the initial period after World War II, congressional authority over security policy depended heavily on the advice of military experts. Before the explosion of congressional staffs in the 1970s, there were few security policy experts in Congress. As Raymond Dawson noted: "The task confronting Congress in acting upon this [defense] budget is overwhelming. Its members have, and can have, no adequate facilities for formulating alternative programs in any systematic fashion; *for this they must rely on military dissent*" (emphasis

[28] See Kiewiet and McCubbins (1992).

[29] For a discussion of the effectiveness of this policy with regards to weapons procurement, see McNaughter (1989).

[30] Reis (1964), Stephens (1971).

[31] From the perspective of military and congressional elites, the National Security Council was designed to avoid the pattern of the highly personalized ad hoc decision-making style Roosevelt had used during World War II: "The president was, to some, a 'rogue elephant' who needed fencing in, or perhaps in Truman's case, a 'weak reed' in need of shoring up. Such concerns were widely shared. The report of the Hoover Commission Task Force of January 1949 saw Presidential participation in the conduct of foreign policy as 'marked with many pitfalls,' and emphasized that 'the president should consult his foreign policy advisors in the executive branch before committing the U.S. to a course of action'" (Nelson 1981, p. 232).

[32] Sec. 202(c) (6), *National Security Act, Act of August 10, 1949*, 63 Stat. 575, quoted in Huntington (1957), p. 416.

added).[33] In its quest to have access to dissent, Congress resisted reforms to the National Security Act that would have eliminated interservice rivalry.

The institutionalization of a positive role for Congress in the creation of military policy also heightened the competition among the civilian branches of government. Intuitively, one might expect that the competition between both the services and the civilian branches would lead to a broad range of military doctrine, or strategic pluralism.[34] In fact, it did not. Each military institution was eager to gain the most benefit from this new international role for the United States. However, in the postwar period, this meant minimizing the cost of demobilization. The budgetary parsimony induced each service branch to articulate a strategic mission that was absolutely vital to U.S. security in order to ensure appropriations. To best articulate such a mission, the primary aim of each service was to predict, and prepare to fight, World War III.[35]

The focus on World War III was solidified by the priorities of postwar *grand strategy.* The fundamental threat to U.S. interests (given the bipolarity of the postwar world) was the threat of Soviet expansion. The Soviet Union was the only country with the military means to pose a serious threat to U.S. territory. Its communist ideology, which U.S. policymakers read as bent on expansionism, increased the concern over that threat. The strategy for meeting the threat, the containment doctrine, was based on the rationale that the prevention of communism was desirable but was conditional on the costs and merits of each case. Marginal communist expansion was not worth preventing if it either started a nuclear war or jeopardized American security by spreading U.S. forces too thin; wider balance of power considerations had to be weighed in each case. The implication for policy was that rather than automatically meeting threats with force, the United States should assign priorities and limits to each case and preserve and expand limited war capabilities.[36]

The first priority of the containment doctrine was the containment

---

[33] Dawson (1963), p. 277.
[34] Huntington (1957) makes this argument; see pp. 418–27.
[35] For a supporting analysis, see Huntington (1965), pp. 303–5.
[36] Betts (1977), p. 86.

of communism in Europe.[37] Given the ambiguities in the other priorities, the European and North American theaters were the safest to plan for, the best for making sure plans were carried out, and the least likely to face budget cuts. This focus on Europe was important because it reinforced the Army's embedded bias. That bias, based on European (particularly Prussian) experience, had been solidified by the experiences of World War I and World War II. The bias was embedded in the reward system for Army leaders. The Army's reward system emphasized service in Europe and in conventional style campaigns and accented timeless principles and the incorporation of new technologies.[38] Elite officers in the Army generally came from the combat arms—infantry, artillery, armor, or airborne. Unsurprisingly, they preferred conventional strategic concepts and division-, brigade- or battalion-size operations.[39]

Although the containment of communism clearly articulated the importance of conflicts outside of Europe, Army leaders who had reached the upper echelons were likely to have emphasized Europe in their careers and were likely to see a focus on Europe as important for winning new resources for the Army in its competition with the other service branches. Thus, the risk-averse strategy was to continue to prepare for a conventional, European war.[40]

Quite possibly, had the Army had a different bias before World War II, it might have seen small or unconventional wars as the perfect task for a branch almost eclipsed by the nuclear revolution. In the event, however, it saw police actions and unconventional wars as outside the missions of a professional army. Because this bias was institutionalized through the promotion policies in the Army, which

[37] There was, however, an "Asia-first" clique built around theater commander Douglas MacArthur (ibid., pp. 81–84).

[38] See Krepinevich's discussion of the "concept" (1986, pp. 4–7). See Betts (1977), p. 127.

[39] Betts (1977), p. 131.

[40] The focus on World War III was not isolated to the Army. The Navy tended to downplay the importance of less conventional missions such as its "brown water" tasks in Vietnam (patrolling the rivers), and the Air Force has continually focused on strategic bombing and downplayed more mundane tasks, such as troop support. None of the major service branches had the incentive to prepare for a less important war. Only the players without a chance in the main game (the most unimportant players, by definition) had the incentive to focus on, or remain flexible to, any other threats. See the discussion of the Marines in Chapter 4.

rewarded service in the European theater and in conventional capacities, advocates of unconventional capacities rarely reached positions of prominence in the Army.

The behavior of the military in the first containment war in Korea demonstrates the dominant attitude in the services toward limited wars: they were a chance to practice for the real thing. "The Navy was happy to demonstrate its uses in land warfare and overseas operations; the Army, the indispensability of the foot soldier; the Air Force, its air superiority over the enemy."[41] But none of the services saw Korea as the kind of war they existed for. The Vietnam War provided a more painful and dramatic example of the impact of the Army's preferences on its behavior.

Though the Army's bias was important for the way it reacted to the security demands of the post–World War II era, congressional budgetary policy rewarded and reinforced this bias. The logic of delegation in the United States explains how the Army's budgetary strategy after World War II intensified its focus on the anticipated World War III and on the mass concentrations of men, sophisticated weaponry, and firepower that was expected to be important in that type of war. The competition between Congress and the president over the control of the military made the president's most effective tool for generating change in the reluctant Army—control over personnel—politically risky. The incentives offered by congressional budgetary powers inadvertently reinforced the Army's bias—hence its resistance to presidential intervention of any kind.

In this situation, the institutional model would lead us to expect the president to use micromanagement to change the Army's focus. It also leads us to expect that the Army should be successful in resisting presidential attempts to change or broaden the its concentration. The more expert the president in defense policy, the more successful micromanagement should be; but overall, Army leaders' expertise, allowing them to set the agenda and often control the information available to civilian leaders, also allows them to resist or alter new civilian goals.[42]

[41] Hammond (1961), p. 250.
[42] Lori Gronich's (1989) model of cognitive processing based on "cognitive misers" makes predictions about foreign policy outcomes dependent on the relative expertise of the president. This model works pretty well in the U.S. case for precisely the

Because of this successful resistance, the United States lacked the type of military doctrine necessary for the effective resistance to communist expansion in the Third World that its grand strategy called for. This was not an altogether bad outcome. A focus on decisive victory in the most important theaters guaranteed American security. The arrangement made use of the most effective oversight that Congress and the president could agree upon, in return for which it sacrificed flexibility. However, because U.S. grand strategy depended on flexibility and the United States chose to fight limited wars, this doctrinal rigidity proved costly to the United States.

## Development of Civil-Military Institutions in Britain

The pattern of political competition grew differently in Britain than in the United States. Unlike the U.S. Constitution, modern parliamentary institutions in Britain were not founded but grew out of parliamentary resistance to weak absolutist rule. Parliamentary failure to control the highly organized New Model Army after the English Civil War led civilians in Parliament to adopt strategies that kept the Army unorganized later in the game. The disorganization of the Army kept it from being able to take advantage of divisions in civilian rule during the eighteenth and nineteenth centuries. In order to play one civilian branch off another, the Army must have some degree of integrity. The British Army failed to develop this integrity because of the way parliamentary leaders chose to control the Army. Specifically, the purchase of commissions and the lack of a structured education program hindered the formation of professionalism and professional ties to the Army and thus prevented the formation of uniform preferences before the 1870s.

These difficulties were part of Parliament's strategy for controlling the Army. Having failed to control the highly organized Army after the English Civil War, Parliament's strategy for controlling the Army was to staff it with leaders representative of Parliament, that is, gentlemen of the land. The most important qualification for both

---

institutional reasons I have examined. Interestingly, the relative expertise of decision makers is unimportant in different institutional structures. Lord Salisbury's lack of expertise did not preclude military adaptation in the Boer War.

entry and advancement for Army officers was their social class. No military education was thought necessary. Officers were supposed to be gentlemen first and fight wars only when duty called. The Army was essentially dismantled after each war as the officers returned to their gentlemanly activities. Officers identified themselves with their social class, rather than with the Army. This strategy reduced the possibility that the Crown could use the Army to repress parliamentary rights. However, it also diminished the potential for the Army to develop the organizational integrity necessary to act as a political player.

During this period, there was a high degree of divergence between different officers' doctrinal preferences and capabilities, which contributed to highly variable performance by the Army. Effective action by the British Army was heavily dependent on the personal qualities of particular leaders. It took premier leadership capabilities to impose order on the upper echelons of the Army's administration. An extraordinarily gifted military leader like the Duke of Marlborough could make the system work, but the Army often floundered under less committed generals.[43] The variety of British performance in the period between the American Revolution and the Crimean War is a testament to the power of personal idiosyncrasies in this type of system.[44] Parliament's strategies for ensuring that the military would not act against their interests had inhibited the military from developing either integrity or biases. The trade-off was an unprofessionalized army with highly variable leadership.

Changes in the nineteenth century centralized in the Cabinet all power over policy-making (Cox 1987). As the vestiges of royal control over the Army were removed, Parliament allowed the Army to become professionalized.[45] Largely in response to the performance of the Prussian Army in the 1860s, three major reforms in Britain's military structure were undertaken by the secretary of state for war, Edward Cardwell, under William Gladstone's liberal administration

[43] Barnett (1970).

[44] Ibid.

[45] The Cardwell reforms simultaneously removed the final vestiges of the Crown's control of the Army and instituted the beginnings of professionalization. See Barnett (1970), Beckett and Gooch (1981), Biddulph (1904), Bond (1960, 1961), Omond (1933), Spires (1980).

in the 1870s. These reforms took away any royal authority over the Army outside of parliamentary action, established a new system of service and reserves, and abolished the purchase of commissions. The changes opened the way for a more professionalized Army.[46] By this time, however, the structure of Parliament and the Cabinet, which unified civilian rule, made the oversight process less complicated.[47] The ease with which the Cabinet could intervene in military policy affected the development of military professionalism in Britain.

Within the Army, there were three major schools of thought in the late nineteenth century: *traditionalists* rejected the need for professionalism and were highly suspicious of the Cardwell reforms; *continentalists* and *imperialists* both endorsed the need for modernity and professionalism in the British Army but saw military needs quite differently.[48] In particular, the continentalists resembled the military professionals in the United States. They were infatuated with Prussian military tactics and attempted to develop a science of strategy based largely on the Prussian experience.[49] However, they had very little influence on military policy in Britain. Though they were certainly involved in advocating the Cardwell reforms, their practical significance waned in the next quarter-century: "their failure to pay due attention to the needs and functions of an im-

---

[46] For more information on the Cardwell reforms, see Biddulph (1904), Bond (1961), Cole and Priestley (1936), Omond (1933).

[47] The rapid expansion of the electorate in the nineteenth century increased the number of contested seats in Parliament and prompted candidates to outline policy differences rather than relying exclusively on patronage (which was cost-prohibitive with such a large electorate). The increasing activity of the members of Parliament (in large part caused by the policy focus) led to a crush of legislation, to which the solution was the centralization of authority over policy in the Cabinet. As the importance of the Cabinet grew, party orientation in the electorate grew because the way to influence the Cabinet (and thus policy) was to vote for a member of Parliament from a particular party. See Cox (1987).

[48] This discussion is based on Bailes (1981).

[49] Two notable examples of thinkers in this tradition are Colonel Lonsdale Hale and F. N. Maude. See Bailes (1981), pp. 31–32. Hale specialized in the minute dissections of the great battles in the Franco-Prussian war and abstract, stylized schemes of attack and defense. His prescription for military thinkers was to study the German experience, "page by page, paragraph by paragraph, line by line." See Hale (1876). Maude, too, assumed that the Prussian victories of 1866 and 1870 portrayed the art of war in perfection. He was concerned with the British tendency toward timidity and advocated offensive, massed operations. See Maude (1907, 1908).

perial army meant a steady decline in their influence up on its development."[50]

The imperialists had much more influence on military policy in Britain. Although they, too, looked to the continent for lessons, they tended to modify these lessons to deal with the particular and immediate problems that Britain faced. Colonel George Furse, the Army's chief expert on logistics wrote, "Our wars differ so essentially from the wars carried out by Continental armies, that we should not adhere to a servile imitation of their systems, but we should originate one of our own which may be in consonance with our requirements."[51] To do this, the advocates of this view developed a critical attitude toward the lessons of the Prussian experience, espoused a doctrine in which the Army's primary role was imperial policing and home defense, and practiced a progressive attitude toward officer education and technological innovation.[52]

The imperialist views had the most effect on British military policy in the later part of the nineteenth century because it was easy for unified civilian leaders to select officers who held (what leaders thought were) the most reasonable policy prescriptions for national security problems. The military leaders who advocated the policy best able to meet civilian interpretations of the demands of Britain's grand strategy were appointed by politicians in the War Office.[53]

---

[50] Bailes (1981), p. 31.

[51] Ibid., p. 37.

[52] Ibid.

[53] George Chesney, Earl Russell, and Sir Garnet Wolseley were among the most prominent of this school. There was some debate over the details of the Army's mission within this group. As Wolseley struggled for a dominant position in the Army in the late 1880s, he capitalized on British fears of invasion. He argued that the Army should pay more attention to home defense. Wolseley had a political incentive for making this argument. He was involved in a contest with the "India school"— led by Lord Roberts—which believed that India was in greater danger of an invasion from Russia than Britain was of an invasion from France. Had the Army garnered a more important role in the defense of Britain, Wolseley would have solidified his control over a more prestigious Army and, at the same time, opened the door for greater budgetary allocations.

Wolseley's perspective on national defense, however, threatened the Navy's role as the first line of defense. The Navy had always held that successful invasion was best deterred by command of the sea. Politicians settled this debate by allocating £21,500,000 for improving naval forces in the Naval Defense Act of 1889. The Navy was to build 8 battleships, 38 cruisers, and 22 gunboats. The Army was given a mere £600,000 as consolation. Although remnants of this debate over the role of the Army

Because the British Army, unlike the U.S. Army, became profession-alized under conditions of easy civilian intervention, Army purists were not able to set the agenda as to what counted as war. If their theories did not address the problems that Britain faced, they were ignored. Those Army officers who did focus on the more flexible doctrine that Britain's grand strategy demanded were rewarded with appointments in the War Office. Military leaders had every reason to pay close attention to civilian goals and to create military doctrine that would meet them. Military leaders had incentives to be flexible to civilian goals.

Because the British Army became professionalized under close civilian scrutiny, its training and promotion tracks reflected civilian concerns. There was little chance for the continental school to become dominant in the Army as long as civilians, who were interested in solving immediate threats, affected promotion patterns. Because officers were rewarded for success in meeting immediate threats, they had an incentive at the end of the nineteenth century, to develop a uniquely British military doctrine emphasizing adaptability.

The Cabinet—particularly the secretaries of state for war—exercised clear control over military personnel. Because their control over military personnel was not politically costly, politicians did not have to bother themselves with trying to micromanage British military doctrine. The fact that they could easily replace personnel who did not produce the desired results acted to keep military leaders closely attuned to civilian leaders' preferences for a flexible army.

The political incentives of members of Parliament (MPs) left few avenues for disgruntled continentalists. As Parliament adjusted to the reforms in the nineteenth century, the structure of party-controlled electoral games left fewer openings for the pork-barrel

in home defense continued for the next decade or so, the Army gradually became converted to the "blue water" school. By 1895, most had accepted the Navy's claim that it could provide effective defense from invasion.

Incidentally, after the Boer War, Lord Roberts also capitalized on the invasion threat. He was trying to introduce conscription. His strategy was to use the fear of invasion but undermine the Navy's claim that it could provide the best defense in order to argue for the rapid introduction of the draft. See Gooch (1981), pp. 7–11.

connections that we saw in the U.S. case.[54] Members of Parliament were nominated for office by party lists, not district primaries. Politicians in Parliament did pay attention to concerns that affected their (more precisely, their party's) political fortunes—the avoidance of high taxes and wars—but politicians interested in their party's fortunes, rather than their district's, are less open to lobbying about the political costs of cutting bases or weapons systems.[55] The Army had little opportunity in this situation to establish a strategic mission or increase its resources. Instead, it was required to mobilize quickly only when war became unavoidable.

Without institutional divisions in the civilian leadership, there was no opportunity for rigid doctrinal biases to develop. No one with any power had a stake in any particular doctrine. Army leaders had no way of carving out spheres of discretion over things like the measurement of success or the limits of warlike behavior such as they might have used to enhance a bias toward particular doctrinal responses. As the British Army became professional, it did not reflect the same fixation on deductive principles that we saw in the U.S. Army. Its leaders had less attachment to offensive, massed movements and less resistance to change.[56]

The British Army also reflected different organizational characteristics than did the U.S. Army. Even after the Boer War, when initial British failures, combined with increasing worries about German power on the continent, led politicians to pay more attention to the continentalists, the ability of unified civilian leadership to direct military performance led the Army to reflect civilian concerns.[57] The

---

[54] See Cox (1987). Shugart and Carey (1992, pp. 7–9) contrast the efficiency of the British-type system with the representativeness of systems more closely based on geography or narrow interests.

[55] For the difference between political corruption in the United States and Britain, see Johnston (1993).

[56] Some have argued that the British Army manifested an antipathy to anything that required offensive, massed movements. See Bidwell and Graham (1982), p. 3.

[57] British concern with Germany was not new. It had contributed to the passage of the Cardwell reforms in the 1870s, and the British had continued to keep an eye on German strength through the end of the century. In fact, initial reaction to the Boer threat was predicated on what effects the reaction would have on the British relationship with Germany. As Lord Esher put it: "there is no doubt that within a measurable distance there looms a titanic struggle between Germany and Europe for mastery. The years 1793–1815 will be repeated, only Germany, not France, will be trying for

increasing focus on the continent was an artifact of civilian concern. Even as Britain instituted reforms that increased the institutional integrity and coherence of the Army and opened new possibilities for the defense community to advise politicians, the prime minister retained politically risk-free control over personnel.

In 1902, the Committee of Imperial Defense (CID) replaced the old Cabinet Defense Committee. The committee included military personnel as equal members of the defense committee. By integrating military experts into the committee, reformers thought they could induce the experts to speak more freely without being so likely to incur the displeasure of their departmental heads. Still, because membership on the committee was flexible and entirely the choice of the prime minister, it solidified ultimate civilian control. In addition, the CID remained true to the notion of collective responsibility. All executive decisions rested on the Cabinet, and all executive action remained with the departments.[58]

In 1903, the War Office (Reconstitution) Committee—the so-called Esher Committee—was appointed to examine the organization of defense in light of the Boer War. The results of these proposals created a more professional advisory body on Army matters and a secretariat responsible to the prime minister that would anticipate the needs of the prime minister and CID. The reorganization initiated an Army Council similar to the Board of Admiralty to serve as a professional advisory body to the Cabinet. The Army council included the quartermaster general, the adjutant general, the master general of the ordnance, and the finance minister (a civilian). Each had access to the Cabinet minister who chaired the council (the secretary of state for war).[59] The council was intended to be a strategy department like the German General Staff, such as could create coherent Army responses to Britain's defense problems.

Also, a permanent and powerful advisory organization (a secre-

---

European domination. She has 70,000,000 of people and is determined to have commercial pre-eminence. To do this England has got to be crippled and the Low Countries added to the German Empire" (quoted in Craig and George 1983, p. 42). After the turn of the century, the Entente Cordial with France and the Anglo-Russian agreement of 1907 represented British actions on this belief.

[58] The CID was purely an advisory committee. See F. Johnson (1960), pp. 56–59.

[59] The appointment of a commander in chief was abolished. See Bidwell and Graham (1982), p. 46; Hart (1939), pp. 249–50; F. Johnson (1960), pp. 62–63.

tariat to the prime minister) was established to gather and collate information on which to base war policy and make peacetime preparations. The secretariat would not simply wait for requests from the Cabinet for information but could inform the prime minister of pressing matters as it saw fit.[60] This mechanism sought to alleviate the concern that decisions about security preparedness were often left to the whims of the prime minister.[61] An institutionalized system of military advice, it was thought, would ensure against military disasters: "There have been in the past, and there will be in the future, Prime Ministers to whom the great questions of Imperial Defence do not appeal. . . . It is not safe to trust matters of national security to the chance of a favorable combination of personality characteristics."[62] The secretariat was to provide the continuity that would ensure that planning would go on regardless of the personal characteristics of the minister in power.[63]

Because the secretariat operated under the absolute power of the prime minister, however, there was little opportunity for it to carve out discretion outside the prime minister's purview:

> It was to the secretariat that the Prime Minister would naturally turn when he desired information or understanding upon which to base a case at variance with that which his departmental expert was presenting. These secretaries were themselves professional officers, and hence possessed of opinions on these matters. There was obviously some danger here of the development of a body competing with the service departments, but, with one lapse in 1907, there seems to have grown up in the secretariat a remarkable loyalty to the Prime Minister, and freedom from either service bias or encroachment upon departmental responsibilities.[64]

After these reforms, one might argue that Britain in World War I exhibited exactly the kind of inflexible fixation on the offensive that

[60] F. Johnson (1960), pp. 63–65.

[61] For a discussion of the development of collective responsibility in the United Kingdom, see Cox (1990).

[62] *Esher Journals*, vol. 2, p. 5, quoted in F. Johnson (1960), p. 65.

[63] The secretariat had three duties: the preservation of the records of the CID, the procurement of information for the CID, and the provision of a continuity of method in treating questions coming before the CID.

[64] F. Johnson (1960), p. 66. In the reference to 1907, Johnson is speaking of George Clark, who, in his actions as secretary, interpreted his duties too widely and was

organizational theory expects, despite unified civilian control. Indeed, many argue that Britain's offensive behavior in World War I rivaled, if it did not equal, the inflexibility displayed by her continental counterparts.[65] Why, if these reforms did not undermine central control over personnel, did the British not react more flexibly to the threat in World War I?

First, we must be careful not to lump the British in the same category as the continental armies. Unlike the military leaders on the continent, leading British military personnel did not subscribe to beliefs about the possibility of quick and decisive offensive strikes. In fact, in 1909, Kitchener stated that a war with Germany would take at least three years. His long-term vision for British security was based on, and expected, a long war.

> Kitchener's New Armies were not designed to play a major part in the land fighting. He raised them to insure that Britain won the peace. British strategy in the opening months of the war bore marked similarities to the policies pursued by Pitt the Younger in the 1790s. Asquith and his colleagues launched a series of expeditions to capture Germany's colonies both to protect British oversees possessions and trade routes and in the hope that they would be able to use them as bargaining counters at the peace conference. They sought allies in Scandinavia, in the Mediterranean and in the Balkans in order to isolate the central powers and in the hope of throwing the burden of the land war still further onto the shoulders of others.[66]

Believing that a war with Germany would last at least three years, Kitchener's intention was for British strength to reach its height after the other powers had battered each other to a standstill. Then the British would be the ones to deliver the final blow to Germany in order to dictate the terms of peace.[67]

Both alliance considerations and strategic goals, however, increasingly drew Britain toward both participation in the land war and, eventually, the pursuit of offensive doctrine, as was most clearly

---

removed when he advised the prime minister to oppose Fisher's construction of Dreadnoughts, which was supposedly a purely naval matter (ibid., p. 74).

[65] See, esp., Travers (1987).
[66] French (1986), p. 20.
[67] Ibid., p. 26.

evidenced in the battle of the Somme. Britain's plans to remain aloof were regarded with suspicion, especially in Russia (where it was rumored that the British would fight to the last Russian) but also in France. British support for the French tried to walk a fine line, sending enough troops to keep the French satisfied but trying to pursue a strategy of attrition that would minimize British casualties.

The casualties that the German army inflicted on the French and the Russians increasingly demonstrated to Britain that she would have to bear more of the military burden if there was to be a decisive defeat of Germany. And a decisive defeat of Germany was what British politicians had decided upon. Germany's decision to launch a strike was quickly identified by Britain as evidence that a militaristic faction including the crown prince, Admiral Alfred von Tirpitz, and the Army had deliberately sought war. The British insisted that they were fighting a crusade "to free Belgium from German domination, to uphold the rights of small nations, and to eradicate Prussian militarism from the fabric of German politics."[68] The only truly satisfying outcome would be a democratic transformation of Germany. However, civilian leaders were unwilling to allocate the resources necessary to create an Army capable of inflicting the resounding defeat necessary to bring about such changes.[69] Britain sought grandiose goals with limited means—means that left Britain out of the doctrinal driver's seat in the first two years of the war. British military leaders could not control the strategy of battles in which they were only providing limited support.

Thus, Britain did not exhibit either the unfounded optimism or obsession with offense that her continental counterparts did before World War I. Yet, the limited means that British politicians sought to use left the British military constrained to support the offensive tactics of her continental allies in the first two years of the war. The grandiose ends of British grand strategy, once the war began, prevented the British from thinking about a negotiated solution.

Nonetheless, the record shows that a profound belief in the offensive spirit was indeed a factor in the British execution of war plans, especially after 1916.[70] It was civilian leaders, in the period before

[68] Ibid., p. 22.
[69] Ibid., p. 23.
[70] Travers (1987).

and during World War I, who desired a strategy to meet continental aims and appointed officers reflecting this perspective.[71] Those scientific officers who were left out of the policy process in the late nineteenth century were brought in after the reforms precipitated by the Boer War. These officers undoubtedly pursued their interests in creating an orientation in the army more akin to the Prussian model. Their influence on doctrine, however, was dependent on approval by civilian leaders.[72]

The same mechanisms (notably, politically risk-free control over personnel) which kept more scientific soldiers from having much effect on policy toward the end of the nineteenth century allowed offensive-minded civilians quickly to begin rewarding offensive, rather than adaptive, behavior. The same control over personnel that, during the Boer War, inadvertently spurred adaptation was equally effective spurring offensive *action* (if not *thinking*) during World War I.

The British Army, however, never developed the agenda setting power over doctrine that the U.S. Army has held in the twentieth century. Divided civilian control over the Army in Britain in the eighteenth and nineteenth centuries had different results than in the United States because Parliament was worried that any army could be used as a tool for royal resurgence, and that an organized Army could be as dangerous to parliamentary power as was the Crown. Instead of trying to check executive power by making the Army more autonomous and professionalized, Parliament limited the usefulness of the Army by keeping it small and disorganized. Beliefs that a maritime strategy relying heavily on sea power could defend Britain's absolute security and the availability of foreign mercenary forces legitimized this strategy.

When the Army began to become professionalized, the secretary of state for war had formal, as well as effective, control over military administration, promotions, appointments, and the like. This power made commanders in the field more sensitive to the preferences of the Cabinet. Policy-making dynamics in the Parliament, which reduced the role of pork barrel and elevated the importance of party

---

[71] McDermott (1979).
[72] Travers (1987).

and the Cabinet for electoral considerations, reinforced the trend toward a smaller, more flexible and efficient Army.

All of this led Great Britain toward a very different response to its hegemonic position in the international system than the United States' response that we saw earlier. With no well-connected domestic interests to push for an effective continental strategy, the British military in the nineteenth century rode their reputation as far as it would take them. When threats did arise, they mobilized quickly to meet them, though usually not quick enough to keep them from losing the first battles. This flexibility had other costs, as well. If the British Army was much less likely to misunderstand the unconventional tactics of a peripheral foe, it was more likely to suffer from the misjudgments of political leaders, with the result that it was often ill prepared to deal immediately with the military might of conventional enemies.[73]

Using institutional logic, we can predict general tendencies about the development of military biases. Military organizations are more likely to have different preferences than do civilian leaders if they professionalize themselves relatively free from civilian interference, and this is more likely to happen when civilian leadership is divided.[74] Conversely, military organizations are more likely to have similar preferences to civilian leaders if civilian leaders exercise strong control over the organization during its professionalization, which is more likely to happen when civilian leadership is unified.

We are likely to see militaries respond flexibly to civilian goals if (1) the organizations are professionally biased toward flexibility or (2) civilians can exercise control over personnel relatively free from political costs. (Control over personnel both allows civilian leaders to select more innovative or flexible military leaders and induces military leaders to pay attention to civilian goals.) Oversight mechanisms other than personnel can promote change but are more prone to adverse side effects.

To make more precise predictions about the preferences or behav-

[73] This is similar to what Huntington calls "subjective civilian control" (1957, pp. 80–81).

[74] I have not used institutional theory to explain why Prussian ideas were so prevalent in the late nineteenth century. Other analysts, working from a similar framework, have examined how ideas become dominant. See Spruyt (1991).

ior of a particular military organization, however, we must look at the historical development of that organization. The institutional model is more useful than classical organizational models because it allows us to look specifically at the development of an organization to determine its preferences and thus allows us to notice differences between the attitudes of different military organizations to change. Although it requires more historical inputs, the focus on oversight limits the amount of history necessary to understand the preferences and behaviors of military organizations.

International forces are important not because they are determining but because they affect the strategies of domestic players. Thus, a hegemonic position per se does not yield any predictions about the type of military organizations that will appear. Similar international positions prompted very different military organizations and civil-military relations in these two cases. Nonetheless, the change in the United States' international position was very important in propelling Congress toward taking a greater role in defense policy-making, which had a large impact on both civil-military relations and military behavior.

# [3]

# *Vietnam:*
# *Why the Army Failed To Adapt*

The U.S. Army's doctrine in Vietnam was not integrated with the nation's grand strategy. Army leaders did not create a doctrine appropriate for achieving American ends in Vietnam. "There is 'no evidence of institutional learning in the services' as regards this kind of war, no understanding of the differences between the constraints of small war and America's current 'offensive, give-them-everything-you've-got military doctrine.'"[1] Chapter 2 explained the roots of the Army's bias toward a particular type of war. The present chapter explains why the Army resisted change even when presidents urged its leaders to adopt a doctrine better suited to American goals in Vietnam.

There were two main reasons why the U.S. Army did not adapt to the enemy in Vietnam. The first has to do with the mixed signals the Army received from civilian leaders. While presidents were urging the Army to adopt a counterinsurgency capability, congressional budgetary policy induced the Army to focus on Europe. The second has to do with the reward structure in the Army. The Army's bias toward big wars in Europe was instilled through a structure that most consistently rewarded those officers who focused on big wars in Europe and those who played by the book. So while Kennedy, and then Johnson, urged the Army to adopt counterinsurgency doctrine, both the structure of Army promotions and the Army's budg-

---

[1] Cohen (1986), pp. 296–97, quoting Bowden (1982), p. 62.

etary goals interacted to provide strong incentives for Army leaders to ignore these urgings.

Presidents faced constraints in their use of personnel to change the Army's focus. Those Army leaders who had reached high ranks generally had similar backgrounds and preferences. To garner change, the president would have to reach down into the ranks. This was a politically risky strategy. Presidential appointments had to be ratified by the Senate. Questionable appointments could cause the Army leadership to rally senatorial disapproval. Replacing high-ranking personnel during a conflict, even if largely supported by Congress, presented an opportunity for the president's opponents to raise negative publicity through hearings and the like. As we shall see, presidents, instead, tried less controversial uses of personnel, creating new offices and staffing them with officers committed to counterinsurgency. In addition to being less controversial, however, these tactics were also less likely to prompt appropriate change.[2]

The president could also try to micromanage change. He could order that more time be spent in certain types of training, or that more resources be allocated to different types of doctrine. As we shall see, however, information asymmetry hindered the president and his staff from effectively overseeing the implementation of these changes. The president and his subordinates would have needed a vast amount of both knowledge about military matters and time in order to ensure that the military really made the changes that the president requested.

The most effective oversight mechanism was Congress's power over the budget. The Budget Act of 1921 induced the Army and the Navy to compete with one another over funds. After the postwar reorganization, the Air Force, too, entered the competition over funds to provide national defense. As mentioned in Chapter 2, competition over dollars was also a competition over strategy. For the Army to justify increased funds, it had to show how it provided the first line of defense. The first line of defense provided by the Army looked different from that provided by the Navy, which looked dif-

---

[2] Betts categorizes appointments according to the degree of political consideration. The first category—routine-professional— does not make political compatibility with the administration a central consideration. Forty-three of the 56 appointments that Betts surveys fall into this category. See Betts (1977), pp. 56–57.

ferent still from that provided by the Air Force. In its budgetary allocations, Congress could pick and choose among the strategies presented by each service branch.[3] The services had every reason to pay attention to what would win in Congress in order to ensure their budgets.

This process, however, combined with the postwar national security agenda, induced the service branches to focus on *the most important threat* even as it required them to be ready to meet *a wide variety of threats*. The postwar security agenda was organized around the containment of communism. Within the containment logic, however, there was a wide range of meaning. The most extreme versions preached that the United States was in a struggle against evil with no room for compromise.[4] The more pragmatic renditions argued that the United States' vital interests were in Europe. Other areas were conditional on the costs and merits of each case. Marginal communist expansion was not worth stopping if it started a nuclear war, nor was it worth preventing if it jeopardized American security by spreading forces too thin. Wider balance-of-power calculations had to be made in each case.[5]

Common to both of these was the defense of the United States and Europe. These were priorities so basic that they were assumed throughout the defense community.[6] Regardless of what version of containment was dominant, the United States and Europe always held a primary place. In their competition with one another over budgetary allocations, then, risk-averse service branches had every reason to focus on these theaters. Concern over other theaters might come and go, but North America and Europe were always a safe bet. Only those branches or subbranches whose raison d'être was peripheral to these theaters had any reason to concentrate on doctrine appropriate to other conflicts.

Because the budgetary game reinforced the Army's built-in bias both toward Europe and toward decisive confrontations with major

[3] Ibid., pp. 116–17.
[4] John Foster Dulles's enunciation of "rollback," whereby he advocated the use of any means necessary to secure the liberation of Eastern Europe is an example of the extreme school.
[5] Betts (1977), p. 84.
[6] Gaddis (1987), p. 40; Ross (1989), p. 172. These were priorities shared by both the Congress and the president (especially Eisenhower).

powers, we should not expect the Army to adjust its doctrine to meet unconventional threats. The institutional model would expect Army officers to pursue innovations that would aid them in their quest for promotion—that would be appropriate to the "big war" in defense of the United States and Europe. Particularly when the competition with other service branches for budgetary rewards reinforced this bias, we should expect the Army to resist adopting doctrine appropriate to other types of war in other theaters.

## DWIGHT D. EISENHOWER

American concern with Vietnam began almost immediately after World War II. However, until the time of the French defeat at Dienbienphu, American actions had been restricted to advice and funding. In 1956, United States involvement became more pronounced with the launching of a program to train the South Vietnamese Army.[7] The purpose of this training, according to Secretary of State John Foster Dulles, was to reorganize the Vietnamese Army in such a fashion as to allow it to maintain internal security. Any external threat could be met by the new regional security organization, the South-East Asia Treaty Organization (SEATO).[8]

The Vietnam challenge soon fell victim to the Army's bias. The recent experience of direct invasion in Korea had stimulated a concern throughout the military over a conventional invasion of South Vietnam by the North. This concern reinforced the already-embedded orientation of the Army toward conventional tactics appropriate for a war in Europe. United States aid was directed by the Army toward a strategy to protect South Vietnam from a *conventional attack*. In spite of the fact that all (the Army, the Joint Chiefs of Staff, the Pacific Command Planners, and the CIA) agreed that the most important immediate danger came from subversion,[9] the Army continued to make preparations for a conventional attack by North Viet-

---

[7] Betts (1977), p. 22; *Pentagon Papers* (1971–72), vol. 2, pp. 408, 416.

[8] Memo, ACofs G-3 to G-3 Plans Div, International Branch, 10 Nov. 1954, "Views of Secy of State on Strategy and Force Levels in Indochina," PSYWAR 091 Indochina, cited in Specter (1983), p. 228, n. 35. For the general commitment of U.S. policymakers to internal security, see *Pentagon Papers* (1971–72), vol. 1, p. 266.

[9] *Pentagon Papers* (1971–72), vol. 1, p. 272.

nam the cornerstone of their advisory effort. The assumption was that regularly trained troops would also be capable of performing internal security duties.[10]

Between 1956 and 1960, the U.S. Army's implementation of the training program undermined and eventually changed the program. Instead of creating an army that could maintain internal security, it created one prepared to counter an invasion from North Vietnam. The initial plan submitted by General James Lawton Collins suggested that the South Vietnamese Army could be trained both to maintain internal security and to counter an invasion from the North.[11] The plan was to reduce and strengthen the South Vietnamese Army. Its revamped organization was to have six divisions: three full divisions capable of at least delaying an invasion from North Vietnam and three territorial divisions organized around existing regional commands to provide for internal security and, if necessary, reinforce the field divisions.[12]

The quest for properly trained units to counter the invading force, however, required the battalions to be centralized for training, which disrupted internal security. Most of the units were small and scattered throughout the countryside performing heterogeneous functions against local security threats. The plan was first to centralize the small scattered units, then combine certain units, disband others, and create some new ones. The required centralization left large portions of the population unprotected during the training period. This worried even South Vietnamese President Ngo Dinh Diem and his advisors, who complained that such steps would expose the population now protected by the units to intimidation by the North-Vietnamese-sponsored Vietcong. General John W. O'Daniel, the officer in charge of the training effort, however, argued

[10] Ibid., pp. 272–73. Incidentally, this may be true. Steven Grant (1990) has argued that regular troops can be used for a wide variety of contingencies if they have innovative leadership. Both the U.S. Army and its South Vietnamese trainee, however, had institutional mechanisms that prevented leadership from effectively directing regularly trained troops in the conduct of counterinsurgency campaigns.

[11] Collins was the president's special representative selected to be in charge of the military training program.

[12] Memo, John Foster Dulles to President, 17 Nov. 1954, "General Collins' Recommendations Regarding Force Levels," 751G.00/11-1754, Records of Dept. of State, cited in Specter (1983), pp. 238–39.

that the steps would eventually lead to more internal security as well as the capability to meet external aggression.[13]

The plans also considerably reduced the number of troops serving in South Vietnam.[14] Although these troops were better trained and better equipped, local leaders complained that they were inadequate for carrying out basic security at the local level. Mai Ngoc Duoc, the chief of Long An Province from 1957 to 1961 reproached the central government: "I am sure if you go to the Ministry of the Interior you will still find my reports. I warned them very clearly that if they did not give me enough troops to pacify the province, then whole divisions of troops would not help later on. But they just gave me two Ranger companies. How can you pacify a province with two companies?[15]

In retrospect, O'Daniel's contingency plans were a recipe for worsening internal security problems. First, he pulled units away from the populations they protected. Then, he planned to repel the North Vietnamese by pushing them "off the roads and into the mountainous untracked areas where, if civilians are evacuated from these areas, the enemy [would be] in dire straits."[16] In fact, of course, the enemy's normal area of operation was just where O'Daniel was planning to push him. We can project, even from this point, the

---

[13] Memo, Col. John M. Finn to Gen. O'Daniel, 5 Aug. 1955, "Meeting with Minister of Defense on 4 Aug. 55"; Memo, Gen. O'Daniel to Ambassador Reinhardt, 26 Aug. 1955, "Meeting with President Diem on 24 Aug. 55"; Gen. O'Daniel to Ambassador Reinhardt, 10 Sept. 1955, "Meeting with President Diem, 28 Sept. 1955"—all in O'Daniel Papers, Center of Military History, and all cited in Specter (1983), p. 265; Lt. Gen. Samuel Williams, "MAAG-TERM Activities Nov. 55–Nov. 56," p. 5–7, Samuel T Williams Papers, Military History Institute Archives, cited in Krepinevich (1986), p. 23. I do not suggest that the South Vietnamese Army was performing pacification tasks effectively before U.S. training. The ARVN was riddled with corruption, was poorly trained, and was unable to keep the population safe. I wish to suggest, however, that the general operating procedures of the U.S. Army carried the day over practical concerns about the security of the population.

[14] They were reduced from 170,000 to 77,000. See Memo, John Foster Dulles to President, 17 Nov. 1954, "General Collins' Recommendations Regarding Force Levels," 751G.00/11-1754, Records of Dept. of State, cited in Specter (1983), p. 238.

[15] Race (1972), p. 63. His chapter 2 (from which this quote is drawn) analyses local politics during the training period.

[16] Memo, O'Daniel to Ambassador Reinhardt, 1 Aug. 1955, "Conversation with President Diem," O'Daniel Papers; Williams, "An Estimate of the Situation," 16 Nov. 1955, Folder 6, Samuel T. Williams Papers, Military History Institute Archives; both cited in Specter (1983), p. 268.

problems that the United States would have in engaging the enemy in battle. Looking to push him off the roads, the Army would miss the enemy it wanted to engage. The enemy could operate freely by moving in untracked areas, at night, into populated districts left unprotected by the Army, which was looking to meet the enemy in an offensive stance.

From 1956 through 1961, General Samuel Williams commanded the advisory effort in line with the Army's standard procedures. The result was a Vietnamese Army consisting of seven divisions based on U.S. Army divisional force structure. According to a senior Military Assistance Advisory Group (MAAG) official, it was "a very close parallel on a considerably lighter scale of the division as we knew [it] in World War II."[17] In short, during the 1950s, civilian leaders' instructions to train the South Vietnamese Army to maintain internal security were undermined by Army training officers. In the course of the training, the goal was changed from ability to maintain internal security to ability to repel an invasion from the North Vietnamese.

The Army's bias could not be disrupted by bureaucratic infighting. There was potential for more accurate diagnoses of the situation in Vietnam in agencies not bound by the Army's World War II–biased perception. The Army's corner on military expertise, however, allowed them to discount other agencies' challenges. Also, the bureaucratic rivalries between the other agencies kept them from sharing information or joining to challenge the Army. Without a concerted challenge to the Army's claims, disagreements were often attributed to civilian agencies' lack of military understanding.[18]

## JOHN F. KENNEDY

Kennedy came into office committed to the need for a *flexible response*. He was concerned not only that Eisenhower's notion of *mas-*

[17] Interview with Colonel Dannemiller by Center for Military History (CMH), Washington, 26 Mar. 1980; Starry, (1978), pp. 17–18, quoted in Krepinevich (1986), p. 24; see p. 280, n. 47.

[18] Examples can be found in the clashes between Ambassador Durbrow, head of the "country team" (which included the embassy, the MAAG, the Equipment Recovery Mission, the U.S. Information Agency, the CIA, and the U.S. Operations Mission [a

*sive retaliation* could do little to stop small communist incursions, but also that what conventional forces the United States did have were ill suited for handling brushfire wars in the Third World. Throughout Kennedy's first year in office, he attempted to get the Army interested in counterinsurgency.[19]

Kennedy's campaign to develop counterinsurgency began immediately after he took office. His first step was to try to get the Army interested in counterinsurgency. Promptly after his inauguration, he quizzed his associates about plans for guerilla warfare.[20] The result was National Security Action Memorandum (NSAM) Number 2, which instructed the secretary of defense to investigate an in-

---

field agency of the International Cooperation Administration]) and General Williams, appointed to head the MAAG, clashes that were open and caustic (Specter 1983, p. 276).

Ronald Specter points out that some of these rivalries might have been overcome had there been a coordinating force in Washington. But aside from the president, there was no single authority responsible for the overall direction of the United States effort in Vietnam. The National Security Council (NSC), which was supposed to provide coordination, produced vague and general studies that left the State and Defense Departments free to compete for authority. The U.S. Information Agency, the CIA, and the U.S. Operations Mission maintained their own council in their specialized fields (ibid., p. 277). The lack of a coordinated effort in the United States and in Vietnam left the agency responsible for carrying out the policies (the MAAG) with a large degree of what Richard Betts calls indirect influence (or influence over the implementation of policy that may act to determine its shape) over what actually happened in Vietnam. See Betts (1977), pp. 5–7.

[19] The doctrine that came to be associated with this notion of counterinsurgency is simple and has several defining characteristics. It is defensive, its goal being pacification—defending larger and larger areas against the enemy. It is likened to an inkblot, beginning small and spreading larger and larger as more and more area becomes pacified. Its tactics involve a close association with the population to be protected, which deprives the guerrilla of the protected population's cooperation and makes him retreat to other areas for support. As he retreats, the population is geared for self-defense and the inkblot spreads outward to bring more populated area under protection.

The key to this doctrine is its aim—to deprive the enemy from access to the population. This was very different from what eventually became the aim of U.S. doctrine in Vietnam, namely, to destroy the will of the North Vietnamese to continue fighting. The United States would have been much more likely to achieve the aim associated with a counterinsurgent doctrine. By placing itself in a battle of wills against the North Vietnamese, the United States unnecessarily disadvantaged itself. It was unlikely that American will to fight in a country halfway across the world would be greater than the North Vietnamese will to fight in its own country.

[20] Hilsman (1967), p. 413.

crease in counterguerrilla resources.[21] Shortly following a special message to Congress, where he argued that the nation needed a greater ability to deal with guerrilla forces, insurrection and subversion, Kennedy directed the Army in May 1961, to examine its force structure in light of a possible commitment to Southeast Asia. In November, he summoned high-ranking Army commanders and urged them to back the counterinsurgency program: "I know that the Army is not going to develop this counterinsurgency field and do the things that I think must be done unless the Army itself wants to do it."[22]

The Army responded minimally to Kennedy's appeal.[23] The president's obsession with counterinsurgency was seen as a fad, which the Army should not get caught up in but should satisfy with minimal effort.[24] Kennedy's aides' lack of expertise on military matters hampered the ability of the administration to force the Army into a task which it deemed unimportant. The Army paid lip service to the administration's request while instituting very few actual changes. Furthermore, the changes the Army did make were determined not by what would best counter the insurgent threat, but what could satisfy the president's request and still be applicable to (or at least not detract from) a serious war against the Soviet Union in Europe.

General Lemnitzer (chairman of the JCS from 1960 to 1962) declared that the administration was oversold on the importance of guerrilla warfare. Similarly, General George H. Decker (Army chief of staff from 1960 to 1962) countered a presidential lecture on counterinsurgency with the reply, "Any good soldier can handle guerrillas." General Maxwell Taylor, too, felt that counterinsurgency was "just a small form of war" and that "all this cloud of dust that's coming out of the White House really isn't necessary."[25]

[21] U.S., Department of Defense, *U.S.-Vietnam Relations*, U.S. Government Printing Office, Washington D.C., 1971, vol. 11, p. 17, cited in Blaufarb (1977), p. 52.
[22] Interview with Elvis J. Stahr by Robert H. Farrell, CMH, 18 Aug. 1964, p. 33, quoted in Krepinevich (1986), pp. 31 and 280, n. 10.
[23] Hilsman (1967), pp. 424–25; Krepinevich (1986), p. 33; R. Smith (1983), pp. 56–60. See also Komer (1986).
[24] Rosson (1962), p. 6; U.S. Army Combat Developments Command (CDC), "Doctrinal Literature for Special Warfare" (draft), Jan. 1964, CMH, p. 2, cited in Krepinevich (1986), pp. 40 and 281, nn. 28, 30.
[25] Interview with Maxwell Taylor by Andrew Krepinevich, 17 June 1982, cited in Krepinevich (1986), pp. 36–37, 281, n. 19. It was Maxwell Taylor's *Uncertain Trumpet*

Kennedy responded to the Army's initial resistance by using his powers of appointment. As we would expect, he did not try anything too bold. Replacing the Army chief of staff with a counterinsurgency specialist, for example, would have been politically risky. Instead, he created new posts staffed with counterinsurgency experts who could spearhead his movement. He appointed Brigadier General Rosson as special assistant for special warfare to be Army Chief of Staff General Decker's eyes and ears on special warfare activities. General Rosson had a long and distinguished history both in Vietnam and in special warfare.[26] Rosson, however, was given only limited access to the Army force structure. Seen by the Army as a representative of the administration, he was not allowed to develop his own staff and was instructed to focus only on the Army's "special assets" (i.e., the Green Berets and the Psychological and Civil Affairs Units). Any special warfare requirements influencing main force units were kept outside Rosson's supervision.[27]

The Stilwell Report, issued on October 13, 1961, faulted the Army for failing to evolve a simple, dynamic doctrine within the conceptual framework of counterinsurgency.[28] The Howze Board report on special warfare in January of 1962 echoed the Stilwell report's findings. It stated that although the Army had a latent potential for counterinsurgency operations, "neither its indoctrination nor train-

---

that had alerted Kennedy to the need for flexible response. What Taylor envisioned with flexible response, however, was an army capable of waging a mid-intensity conflict. Kennedy took Taylor's ideas to their logical conclusion in the Third World with his push to extend flexible response to low-intensity conflicts. Taylor, however, remained unconvinced of both the need for, and ability of, the U.S. military to engage in low-intensity conflict in the Third World. See Krepinevich (1986), pp. 28–29.

[26] Rosson had also served in the 39th Infantry Regiment Command in Europe and on the JCS for Europe. Interview with General William B. Rosson by Lt. Col. Douglas B. Burgess, William B. Rosson Papers, vol. 2, Military History Institute Archives.

[27] Rosson, (1978), p. 101, cited in Krepinevich (1986), p. 43; see pp. 281–82, n. 41. In addition to the Army's appointment of Rosson, the JCS appointed Marine Major General Victor H. Krulak as special assistant for counterinsurgency and special activities. Krulak was able to mount a serious preparatory effort within the Marines to deal with an insurgent threat. See below at n. 65. For an excellent case study of the Marines' activities, see West (1985). The Marine effort will be examined in detail in Chapter 4.

[28] Memo for the Secretary of the Army from Brig. Gen. Richard G. Stilwell, "Army Activities in Underdeveloped Areas Short of Declared War," 13 October 1961 (hereafter cited as Stilwell Report), pp. vii, xvi, 3, 11–25, 31, 35, 47, 48, 102 (CMH), cited in Krepinevich (1986), pp. 44 and 282, nn. 44–45.

ing is now altogether satisfactory for this mission"; also, much of the counterinsurgency concept, it found, was foreign to fundamental Army teaching and practice.[29]

Although the Army responded to these criticisms with a host of reports, boards, and programs, they were merely a stronger-sounding variant of the lip service that the Army had been paying to counterinsurgency all along. When the administration called for more hours devoted to training for counterinsurgency, Army manuals began to define more activities as counterinsurgency.[30]

Rather than focusing on the new threat, counterguerrilla training came to mean special warfare contingencies within a concept of conventional war. The primary activity focused on was that which had been required in World War II and Korea, the searching out and destroying of guerilla bands.[31] Defined this way, the Army argued that it had been concentrating on counterinsurgency warfare all along. Army Chief of Staff Earle Wheeler said in a speech to the armored division in 1965: "Our division is not a stranger to guerrilla type warfare. In fact, some historians credit troops of the division with originating and perfecting the armored ambush, and the ambush is certainly basic to guerrilla warfare."[32]

The conception of counterinsurgency as a doctrine aimed at denying the enemy access to the population, however, was foreign to General Wheeler's meaning. "Despite the fact that the conflict is conducted as guerrilla warfare," he stated in 1962, "it is nonetheless a military action. . . . It is fashionable in some quarters to say that the problems in Southeast Asia are primarily political and economic rather than military. I do not agree. The essence of the problem in Vietnam is military."[33] The key to the importance of General Wheeler's statement is that it reflects the American Army's limited notion of "military." Because he did not see military action as aimed

[29] USCONARC, Historical Division (1962), vol. 1b, enc. 5, sec. 7, pp. 4–5, 99 (CMH)—cited in Krepinevich (1986), pp. 44 and 282, n. 48.

[30] U.S. Army Command and General Staff College (1959–61, 1963–67). See also Dr. Ivan Birrer to Dr. Dastrup, 23 July 1982 (West Point, N.Y.), cited in Krepinevich (1986), pp. 51, 283–84, nn. 77–78.

[31] Krepinevich (1986), p. 51.

[32] Gen. Earle Wheeler, "From Marchiennes to Bien Hoa" (Speech to Annual Reunion of the 2d Armored Division, Washington), 7 August 1975, in Wheeler n.d., vol. 2, p. 57, quoted in Krepinevich (1986), p. 50.

[33] Hilsman (1967), p. 426.

at denying the enemy access to the population, he did not understand how political and economic factors could influence military outcomes.

Finally, when Kennedy increased the advisory effort in 1962, he appointed Lieutenant General Paul D. Harkins as its commander. Some have argued that the appointment of Harkins was a mistake—that the administration should have chosen a specialist in counterinsurgency, instead of a generalist versed in conventional warfare.[34] The administration did consider Brigadier General William Yarborough and Colonel William Peers—both with backgrounds in counterinsurgency—but feared that the selection of these officers would antagonize the service leadership.[35]

The example of General Rosson demonstrates that these fears were not unfounded. Perceived outsiders faced difficulties working within the Army system.[36] The appointment of Harkins can be seen as an attempt to compromise with the Army (respect its dislike for reaching down into the ranks) in the hopes that an insider could prompt innovation. It could be that Kennedy, having tried the strategy of appointing outsiders and seen it fail, appointed an insider, hoping to convert someone who could work the ropes.[37] General Harkins, however, did not become interested in counterinsurgency.

### Unsuccessful Innovation: The Special Forces

Despite Kennedy's enthusiasm for the Special Forces and the elitism he tried to attach to them, the Army Special Forces never quite

[34] See Krepinevich (1986), p. 65.

[35] Betts (1977), p. 131.

[36] Actually, General Rosson was not even an outsider. He had a distinguished career in the 39th Infantry Regiment Command in Europe as deputy chief of staff for planning and operations, HQ, U.S. Army, Europe under General Abrams and as assistant division commander of the 8th Infantry Division. He had lost favor with Admiral Arthur Radford in his first European experience, however (over a leak on flexible response missile posture). He also had participated in a special course at the Army War College that brought together Army, Navy, Marine, Coast Guard, and civilian personnel designed to prompt interbranch cooperations and understanding. So while he was not an outsider, he was not a run-of-the-mill officer, either. See interview with General William B. Rosson by Lt. Col. Douglas R. Burgess, vol. 2, pp. 228–79, William B. Rosson Papers, Military History Institute Archives.

[37] As Richard Neustadt (1980) has pointed out, this is often an optimum strategy. He argues that the best strategy for presidential success is to bring "outsiders" well

took off in Vietnam. A small contingent of Special Force units did have a promising beginning under the direction of the CIA in the Civilian Irregular Defense Groups (CIDG) program in the early 1960s' but once jurisdiction over the direction of the Special Forces passed back to the Army, the Special Forces began to concentrate on what the Army thought was important. Despite the recommendations of both the Stilwell Report and the Howze Board, that the Special Forces be augmented by regular troops when a conflict became too big, exactly the opposite occurred.[38] As the conflict grew, Regular Army criteria were imposed on the Special Forces, and the Special Force units were subsumed by the Regular Army.

Two dynamics combined to move the Special Forces back under Army control. The first was the desire of lower-level Special Forces leaders to gain more control over (and more offensive direction for) their operations—to make the CIDG program an Army Special Forces program rather than a CIA program. The second was the Military Assistance Command Vietnam's (MACV) interest in controlling and coordinating all action in Vietnam.

---

connected in their own circles into the White House in order to involve them with the administration's goals. Though this policy runs the risk of that the appointment will undermine the administration's policy, its alternative is likely to be worse. By appointing one of the "president's men," the administration would both alienate the outside agency and run the risk that the appointee would encounter resistance from the bureaucracy that he was supposed to command. This, of course, was what happened when Kennedy appointed General Rosson as the Army's special assistant for special warfare.

[38] The Stilwell Report (October 1961) was designed to evaluate the Free-world Liaison and Assistant Group (FLAG) concept with which the Army proposed to meet President Kennedy's request for counterinsurgency forces. Each FLAG consisted of a special forces group; a psychological warfare battalion; and civil affairs, engineer, signal, military intelligence, and medical detachments. The Stilwell Report found that the program was grossly understaffed and that there was little coordination among the different elements of the FLAGs. Stilwell recommended that the Army as a whole be used to meet the counterinsurgency mission.

The Howze Board (December 1961–January 1962) followed up on Stilwell's evaluations. Its report argued that with the worldwide threat of insurgencies, the minimal Special Forces preparations would be inadequate. It argued that existing Special Warfare Groups use the Army as a whole as a reservoir and that detailed planning start to begin training, organizing, and equipping the Army to pursue such a mission. In particular, the board suggested that three divisions and three battle groups be given counterinsurgency as their top priority, and that three other divisions and two other battle groups be given the mission as their second priority. See discussion in Krepinevich (1986), pp. 103–8, and, cited therein, "Stilwell Report," pp. vi, xviii, 3–4, 46–48; "Howze Board," vol. 1a, pp. 13, 31, 47, 49, 53, 102: both in CMH.

Even under the CIA, the Special Forces personnel had demonstrated an undue enthusiasm for the creation of platoon-sized units (strike forces) capable of carrying out offensive strikes against the enemy.[39] There were good reasons for this, given the Army's standards of evaluation, which were biased toward offensive action.[40] Still, in a trip to evaluate the Special Forces in 1962, General Rosson (in his capacity as special assistant to the chief of staff for special warfare) complained about the overemphasis of the strike-force teams and the movement from covert activity to the creation of conventional forces.[41] Both Army leaders with a bureaucratic interest in heightening the Army's role in the conflict, and Special Forces members who were somewhat uncomfortable deemphasizing the offensive spirit that the Army traditionally rewarded had interests in a MACV takeover of the CDIG program.

Once control was passed to the MACV in Operation Switchback, however, the offensive bias of the forces increased. The Army thought that the Special Forces could be better used in an offensive mission. They sought to leave pacification exercises to the local forces and to move the Green Berets into offensive-spirited search-and-destroy missions. Once the Special Forces were under MACV control, it was difficult for them to retain their flexibility and to resist the organizational incentives that undermined their commitment to the idea of a counterinsurgency doctrine.

General Rosson was concerned at the outset about moving the direction of the Special Forces units under the Army and MACV:

> My main concern centered on undertakings reached between the administration and congress in Washington wherein the CIA enjoyed somewhat unique funding authority for covert operations. Under the special authority it was able to create a very flexible logistics system for the arming, equipping, and subsequent supply of montagnard forces and, indeed, for comparable forces that were developed elsewhere in Vietnam. It was my feeling that it was far better to retain the existing CIA logistic support structure and funding apparatus than to create a new system under military auspices. I was convinced in particular that the military, which always had been and continues to be

[39] Rosson (1979), p. 124.
[40] I shall explore this further in Chapter 4.
[41] Rosson (1979), p. 124.

under very strict accounting and budgeting procedures, would not be able to achieve comparable flexibility in the supply and support of these specialized forces among which the CIDG provided the principal example.[42]

When MACV assumed full control over the CIDG from the CIA, it declared that enough strike-force troops had been trained to allow the Special Forces to concentrate on operations directly against the Vietcong.[43] In fact, however, the Vietnamese Special Forces that took over the defense of CIDG villages were ill equipped to assume these responsibilities.[44] By moving too fast and concentrating on "military" problems, Operation Switchback reversed many of the CDIG's initial gains.

The Army wanted to use the Special Forces for unconventional, but not counterinsurgency, missions. Lieutenant General Harold K. Johnson did not see much utility in "simply building little enclaves in each tribal area"; instead, he wanted to see them operating in a manner, "consistent with the unconventional warfare doctrine of mobile, agile forces operating with minimum combat and logistic support."[45]

Even operating under MACV, the Special Forces maintained a stepchild status. Although they became the Army's tool for competing with other branches (particularly the Marines) for counterinsurgency operations, they had difficulties working within the Army bureaucracy. This was due in part to the general distrust with which those who would choose the Special Forces were viewed. As General Johnson put it:

[42] Interview with General William B. Rosson by Lt. Col. Douglas R. Burgess, William B. Rosson Papers, vol. 2, pp. 292–93, Military History Institute Archives. Although the material in this interview is substantiated by General Rosson's rendition of this operation in his dissertation completed in 1979, Andrew Krepinevich reports (based on an interview with General Taylor) Taylor's reminiscence of General Rosson's agreement about the importance of using the Special Forces in an offensive manner. In fact, Krepinevich asserts that Rosson criticized the CIDG forces for their *lack of* offensive operations. I found no evidence to support this assertion.

[43] Krepinevich (1986), p. 73.

[44] Ibid., pp. 72–73; Thompson and Frizzell (1977), p. 250.

[45] Senior Officer Debriefing Interview with Gen. Harold K. Johnson by Col. Rupert F. Glover, 28 Dec. 1972 and 8 and 22 Jan. 1973, pp. ix–27, Harold K. Johnson Papers, Military History Institute Archives.

The Special Forces that were available at the time President Kennedy latched on to them as a new gimmick, were what I would describe as consisting primarily of fugitives from responsibility. These were people that some how or other tended to be nonconformist, couldn't quite get along in a straight military system, and found a haven where their actions were not scrutinized too carefully, and where they came under only sporadic or intermittent observation from the regular chain of command.[46]

The Special Forces also had to withstand more hardships in dealing with red tape for even simple things like obtaining supplies. More importantly, there was great uncertainty over the degree to which promotion benefits were guaranteed to personnel who served in the Special Forces.

General George C. Morton was appointed chief of the Special Warfare Branch Headquarters with the MACV on June 29, 1962. He went to work immediately as a bureaucratic soldier, to win as much of the mission as he could for the Special Forces. He wrote to the Special Forces Office at the Pentagon the day he arrived to let them know that there was a mission the Special Forces should "hop on" immediately unless they wanted the Marines to beat them to it.[47] In a series of exchanges from June through November, General Morton and Ralph Kinnes (at the Pentagon's Special Forces Office) charted their strategy to ensure the enlargement of the Special Forces mission in Vietnam. They were competing against the Marines, who had a counterinsurgency capability; General Harkins and the MACV, who were swayed by the Marines to consider attaching Regular Army units to Marine units; and the Air Force which opposed expanding Army air capabilities to the Special Forces.[48] During this time, however, Morton and the Special Forces headquarters were cut out of the bureaucratic loop for receiving supplies and equipment. Without the activation of a Special Forces Group, there

[46] Senior Officer Debriefing Interview with Gen. Harold K. Johnson by Col. Rupert F. Glover, 28 Dec. 1972 and 8 and 22 Jan. 1973, pp. 8–9, Harold K. Johnson Papers, Military History Institute Archives.

[47] Gen. George C. Morton to Ralph Kinnes, General Staff (GS) (Special Warfare Division, DCSOPS, the Pentagon), 29 June 1962, George C. Morton Papers, Official Correspondence, Personal File, Military History Institute Archives.

[48] Interestingly, although the Special Forces "won" against the Marines, they "lost" against the Air Force and were not allowed to expand the Special Forces air power.

could be no commander, and without a commander, Morton had no authority to order or receive supplies. He was at the mercy of MACV leftovers.[49]

Although Morton was fighting the Marines for a position in the conflict, he was also fighting to remain autonomous from the MACV. There are constant references in the communications between the Washington Special Forces Office and Morton about not letting General Rosson down by becoming part of the MACV.[50] Morton had to walk a fine line between remaining autonomous enough to be distinct from the regular forces and being enough like the regular forces that the Army would support him in competition against the Marines.

Finally, there was a great deal of uncertainty about how a Special Forces tour of duty would affect career patterns. In particular, it was unclear whether or not tours of duty in the Special Forces counted as duty in a troop unit. General Rosson assured Morton in March 1963 that Special Forces tours would certainly not hurt, and would probably help, an officer climb the career ladder: "The Deputy Chief of Staff for Personnel has assured me that duty with Special Forces is considered an approved utilization tour and does not detract from the officer's chances for promotion or for attending the various service schools."[51] In May, however, there was still a great deal of uncertainty. Morton wrote to Colonel George Blanchard: "During numerous interviews with our Special Forces officers, the GPO [sic] stand was that continued assignments in Special Forces would be detrimental to an officer's career. Col. Spears did not consider Special Forces assignment as duty in a troop unit."[52] In a study of Army personnel, Peter Dawkins found that both Special Forces officers

[49] See exchange between Morton and Col. V. V. ("Tex") Laughlin, Department of the Army (DA) (DCSOPS, the Pentagon), 23 and 29 Aug 1962, George C. Morton Papers, Official Correspondence, Personal File, Military History Institute Archives.

[50] Morton to Ralph Kinnes, 19 July and 9 Aug. 1962, and Kinnes to Morton, 3 Sept. 62, George C. Morton Papers, Official Correspondence, Personal File, Military History Institute Archives.

[51] Major General W. B. Rosson to Morton, 29 Mar. 63, George C. Morton Papers, Official Correspondence, Personal File, Military History Institute Archives.

[52] Morton to Col. George Blanchard, 22 May 63, George C. Morton Papers, Official Correspondence, Personal File, Military History Institute Archives.

and Regular Army officers felt that their activities and efforts in unconventional warfare were not evaluated fairly.[53]

Although the Army resisted allocating resources to the Special Forces, if the forces *were* to be a large part of the conflict, the Army wanted to control them. Under Army auspices, however, any latent potential for counterinsurgency among the Special Forces units was ignored.[54]

### Successful Innovation: The Airborne Division

Having documented at length the Army's resistance to counterinsurgency doctrine, I should note that the Army did alter its force structure in the period before American combat troops were committed to Vietnam. The innovation that the Army made, however—the formation of an airmobile division—occurs in precisely the area that the institutional model would expect.

There are three reasons why the introduction of helicopters and the airmobile units were accepted and endorsed by the Army. First, in contrast with the other Special Forces, which were a dead end for anyone who aspired to high rank, the airborne divisions in World War II were an elite corps. Many army leaders in the fifties and sixties were drawn from the "airborne club": Taylor, Ridgway, and Westmoreland served in the same division in 1943.[55] Despite its questionable success in World War II, the airborne divisions continued to be the elite clique in the Army, and the airmobile divisions were enthusiastically endorsed as an extension of this prestigious club.

[53] Dawkins (1979).

[54] At a more mundane level, the Special Forces Headquarters was also subject to the Army's high-tech bias. In one particularly interesting situation, Morton is told of a new audio/visual jeep: "The audio-visual jeep is a mobile training unit mounted in a standard Willy's Jeep Panel truck. The major components of the unit consist of, in addition to the jeep, a 16 mm movie projector, a tape recorder, turn table for playing phonograph records, a slide projector, and a public address set." See Lt. Col. Chester Myers to Morton, Material Activities Division, 16 Jan. 63, George C. Morton Papers, Official Correspondence, personal file, Military History Institute Archives. Morton replies that the audiovisual jeep should be great to train the Vietnamese for civic action. See Morton to Myers, 6 Feb. 1963, George C. Morton Papers, Official Correspondence, Personal File, Military History Institute Archives.

[55] Betts (1977), p. 134.

Second, the airmobile divisions aided the Army in its battle with the Air Force over the provision of close air support of Army field divisions. The Army argued that its own Air Cavalry could provide superior infantry cover and assistance. In so doing, it elevated the prospect of acquiring one more mission for the Army from the Air Force. In 1950, the Army had 668 light airplanes and 57 helicopters; by 1960, it had acquired over 5,000 aircraft of 15 different varieties.[56]

Finally, the doctrine was created for a mid-to-high-intensity conflict, with plans to scale it down for low-intensity conflicts. In order to convince the Army of the importance of airmobility, according to General Howze,[57] it had to work in the European terrain. Harry W. Kinnard, who commanded both the test organization of the airmobility concept and the Army's airmobile division, concurred: "We felt that if we could make it applicable to mid-intensity and high-intensity . . . it would be effective at a lower level."[58]

The airmobile division operated easily within the offensive doctrine that was representative of the Army in general. Army officials argued that it allowed the United States more mobility than the traditional reliance on roads and was thus an advantage in fighting the extraordinarily mobile guerrillas. It allowed the Army to meet the guerrillas and apply massive American firepower on their turf:

The forces for the small war do not require the heavy organizations and equipment with which our forces fought in Korea. This organization and equipment were designed for heavy and sustained warfare in Western Europe, and not for warfare in mountains, jungles, deserts, or other areas of the world (i.e., any place besides Western Europe and the United States) where road systems are limited or missing.

Light forces of high mobility and firepower will answer this requirement. Mobility again becomes the key for the Army's preparation for the contingency of further small wars. This mobility cannot be achieved through minor product improvements in surface vehicles. Only by putting the soldier into a flying machine will we be able to give him superior mobility over indigenous forces, partisans, etc., of the small

[56] Tolson (1973), p. 10, cited in Krepinevich (1956), pp. 114 and 292, n. 45.
[57] Howze was appointed by the Army to reexamine the Army's role in aviation and aircraft requirements. See Krepinevich (1986), p. 119.
[58] USASF, v, Col. John H. Speers, "Commander's Debriefing Letter," CMH, p. 1, cited in Krepinevich (1986), pp. 120 and 287, n. 63.

wars. The required forces, then, for small war appear to be much the same as those for atomic war against the Soviet Union.[59]

By arguing that airmobility could be used similarly in counter-guerilla warfare and in the European theater, the Army could acquire its own air force in Vietnam and use its new capabilities to garner more budgetary allocations in preparation for the defense of Europe. It was a no-lose option for those interested in Army aviation.[60]

By setting up a competition between Army airmobility and traditional Air Force support, the Army managed to avoid the questions about how well airmobility actually worked in the small-war situation. The culmination of the inter-service competition in 1964 demonstrated that Army aviation certainly covered infantry better than did the Air Force. The Air Force offered nothing new or innovative. The competition, however, was exclusively over the protection of infantry in traditional battles, not over innovative ways to conduct counterinsurgency. It was perfectly reasonable, given the choices, for civilian leaders to approve the Army's new mission. The trade-off, however, was not tested in terms of its applicability to the theater where the forces would soon be fighting.[61]

Helicopters did have extraordinary success in the first months of their use in Vietnam. The Vietcong, having never seen them before, panicked and fled. The Vietcong quickly learned the limitations of this technology, however, and took advantage of the advance warning provided by the noise of the airmobile divisions approaching. General Harry W. O. Kinnard acknowledged that the Air Assault units had limited effectiveness in engaging guerrillas: "If the guerrilla chooses to lie low in the jungle . . . it would probably be very difficult to locate him."[62]

---

[59] U.S., Department of Combat Development (1957), cited in Krepinevich (1986), pp. 114 and 292, n. 43.

[60] Not all of the Army's top brass were convinced that helicopters units throughout the force were a good thing. The political interest in preparation for small wars, however, was capitalized upon by the advocates of Army Aviation to further their designs for an Army air force. See Krepinevich (1986), p. 114.

[61] Ibid., pp. 118–23.

[62] Col. Hal D. McCown to DCSOPS, Director of Special Warfare, "Debriefing of Officers Returning from Field Assignments (u)," 10 Oct. 1963, pp. 1, 3, 7, cited in Krepinevich (1986), pp. 125 and 288, n. 84.

Sir Robert Thompson went much further and argued that helicopters were responsible for the failure of American strategy by making possible the mistaken search-and-destroy operations. He argued that mobility was less important than stability for fighting guerrillas. The primary aim of counterinsurgency operations should be to secure the population and ever-greater amounts of territory. Helicopter units allowed Army units to arrive in an area, kill some guerrillas, then leave without securing territory or population. This contributed to already-difficult problems of fighting on behalf of a foreign people by exacerbating the lack of trust between local populations and the U.S. military. In addition, reduced contact between the local populace and the military, drew the Saigon regime even further away from creating political and social credibility at the local level.[63]

In sum, the Air Cavalry, while a successful innovation, was of questionable importance for the counterinsurgency mission. Indeed, it was a successful innovation precisely because it was not designed for the counterinsurgency mission.

## LYNDON B. JOHNSON

After Johnson came into office and then decided to commit troops to Vietnam, the Army did not learn from its mistakes. The search-and-destroy missions that provided the basis for American military doctrine were an offensive attempt to bring as much firepower as possible to bear on the communist forces. The intention was to kill communist forces quicker than they could be recruited, in order steadily to reduce the size of the communist force facing the United States (and the South Vietnamese government). Unfortunately, the execution of this policy disrupted local communities and undermined the security of the population. This made efforts toward nation building—necessary for the ultimate U.S. goal of maintaining a free and independent South Vietnam—much more difficult.

Some have argued that the dual nature of the war (including both attacks by Vietcong insurgents and North Vietnamese main-force units) made it necessary and reasonable for the U.S. forces to con-

[63] See Betts (1977), p. 137; Marr (1971), p. 136; and R. Thompson (1969), p. 136.

centrate on the hard-core northern forces—that light counterinsurgency forces would have been overrun by the heavily armed main forces.[64] Interestingly enough, however, Marine counterinsurgency forces (the Combined Action Platoons or CAP's) in the I Corp area facilitated better results against *both* types of units.

Not only were the Marines able to coordinate resistance to the insurgent strikes, they were also able to gather information about when main-force units would be moving through an area and alert Army forces. Also, when caught by communist main forces, they were able to radio for help much more quickly and efficiently than local Vietnamese forces.[65] The dual nature of the war, in fact, heightened the importance of a coordinated counterinsurgency effort.

Others have argued that the problem with military doctrine in Vietnam was civilian leaders' inability (either because of electoral incentives or owing to the general deficiencies of democracy) to make the hard choices necessary for success. Daniel Elsberg's critique of U.S. policy in Vietnam argues that each president tended to increase the American commitment to Vietnam but without doing what the military deemed necessary to win.[66] He likens American policy-making in Vietnam to a "stalemate machine." Policymakers reacted to two decision rules in the Vietnam conflict: (1) do not lose a country to communism before the next election, and (2) do not commit the United States to a land war in Asia. In trying to follow both of these rules, policy-makers consistently chose the a middle strategy that prevented a win in Vietnam. Kennedy's introduction of advisors, rather than troops, after the 1962 Taylor-Rostow mission is taken to be a landmark case that reinforces this logic.[67] Taylor and Rostow presented Kennedy with three options: pull out, commit more advisors, or commit ground troops. Kennedy chose the middle option.

A variant of this argument is made by Larry Berman with regard to Johnson's decision to commit troops. According to Berman, Johnson refused to consider pulling out of Vietnam because of fears that a foreign policy loss would scuttle his plans for the Great Society

[64] Palmer (1984).
[65] Krulak (1984), Peterson (1989), West (1985).
[66] Elsberg (1971), pp. 217–74.
[67] See Elsberg (1971).

programs. He refused to mobilize popular support behind a war effort because he feared that a national debate on Vietnam would force him to choose between foreign policy goals and domestic policy goals. Johnson did not want to do what it would take to win, nor did he want to lose Vietnam by running away: "And so the decision was made to lose Vietnam slowly."[68]

These arguments are harder to sustain, however, once we realize that Kennedy—and then Johnson—thought the Army's approach was wrong for the situation in Vietnam.[69] Given this opinion, the continuation of the advisory effort along with the sustained attempt to push the military toward innovative solutions in line with counterinsurgency doctrine may have been an *optimal choice* for the Kennedy administration to make. Kennedy thought that committing ground troops to Vietnam would be fighting the wrong kind of war. He did not think the Army's list of options was exhaustive. When a president is trying to get an organization to change, moving slowly makes more sense.

A more sophisticated argument by Leslie Gelb and Richard Betts contends that the system worked in Vietnam.[70] Their reasoning is that (1) the postwar goal of containment of communism was pursued consistently: (2) differences of both elite and mass opinion were accommodated by compromise, and policy never strayed far from the center of opinion both within and outside government; and (3) virtually all views and recommendations were considered—and virtually all important decisions made—without illusions about the odds of success.[71] Foreign policy may have failed, but the decision-making system worked. They go on to assert that democratic governments are "inherently maladapted" to making the kinds of hard choices that would have been necessary to create a foreign policy that would have worked in Vietnam.[72]

Because I am trying to explain military adaptability, not the rela-

[68] Berman (1982), p. 124.

[69] This is an accurate interpretation according to the accounts given by Hilsman (1967), pp. 421–26, and Krepinevich (1986), pp. 61–65. The account in *Pentagon Papers* (1971–72), vol. 2, pp. 115–27, generally supports this view, although the authors state that Kennedy's position cannot be garnered from the official record (p. 117).

[70] See Gelb and Betts (1979).

[71] Ibid., p. 2.

[72] Ibid., p. 4.

tive success of foreign policy or decision-making processes, my argument does not quite contradict the Gelb and Betts analysis.[73] My comparison of the British and American cases suggests, however, that their argument ignores important differences between democracies. Most important, there was more than one middle path in Vietnam. While the middle path pursued by the United States in Vietnam may have led to poor results, a different middle path would have been more appropriate for achieving the United States goals there. Therefore, the inability of democracies to make hard choices may be irrelevant to this case. The development of counterinsurgency would have required neither a decision to withdraw nor a decision to launch a full war in Vietnam, but it would have been a more appropriate doctrine for achieving the military ends of protecting South Vietnam from the communist threat. Whether or not democracies can make hard choices is not the only important variable for explaining military outcomes. The sources of the system in my model—the institutional structure of civilian authority, rather than democracy per se—points to dimensions of the "system" that Gelb and Betts exclude. As will become clear as the comparison between the United States and Britain unfolds, some democracies are better at adjusting military doctrine flexibility to different military challenges than are others.

Fundamentally, however, I agree with a portion of Gelb and Bett's general statement. The problems in Vietnam were problems induced by the system, not by bungling policymakers. Given the electoral circumstances that civilian leaders faced, there were not very good options for inducing the Army to change its bias away from conventional style warfare.

President Johnson, with arguably less expertise in foreign affairs than Kennedy, continued to try to micromanage the military in Vietnam. His intervention in the air war, in particular, has been the subject of much scrutiny.[74] He also, however, continued the tendency to shy away from controversial appointments.

Only after the disasters of the Tet Offensive and the concern this caused in Congress did he remove Westmoreland (by promoting him!). Although Johnson did accomplish some movement on the

[73] For an insightful review of the Gelb and Betts analysis, see Kaiser (1980).
[74] Sharp (1978).

counterinsurgency front with the CORDS program, as I shall discuss in chapter 4, the bureaucratic success of this program depended on its acceptance of Army dominance over the "military" war. As Douglas Blanfarb wrote, Johnson,

> while accepting the rhetoric of his predecessor, did not appreciate the extent to which it remained rhetoric as far as the military establishment was concerned, or that any real change would probably involve a public clash with the army leadership and some forced resignations. If he had, it is doubtful that he would have entertained the prospect.[75]

## CONGRESS

One might have expected to see congressional influence manifested in an overt alliance with the Army to thwart presidential goals. However, both Kennedy and Johnson enjoyed general support in Congress for their activities on behalf of unconventional warfare. Congress seems to have had little active role in the story. However, military leaders *had* turned to Congress and powerful congressional committees to question presidential directions that they opposed in many instances during the post–World War II era. Indeed, Congress was involved in the Army's resistance to the budgetary contractions of the "New Look" under Eisenhower.[76] When Kennedy's—and then Johnson's—flexible response policy reduced the relative strategic importance of the Navy and Air Force, Congress heard these complaints as well.[77] In addition, McNamara's attempts at cost saving were heartily questioned by Congress. In 1966, a House Armed Services Committee report accused McNamara of "almost obsessional dedication to cost effectiveness [which] raises the specter of a decision maker who . . . knows the price of everything and the value of nothing."[78]

So while Congress did not intentionally frustrate presidential influence on the issue of counterinsurgency, congressional actions circumvented presidential success in two ways. First, as mentioned,

[75] Blaufarb (1977), p. 207.
[76] Betts (1977), p. 44; Kolodziej (1966), pp. 200–202, 246–51.
[77] Betts (1977), p. 44; Kolodziej (1966), pp. 323–429.
[78] Quoted in Betts (1977), p. 44.

congressional budgetary decisions were largely allocated on the basis of competition among the services. The biggest part of the pie (and the part least subject to change) was focused on the primary threat. For the Army, this meant the Soviet Union in Europe.[79] The risk-average budgetary strategy induced by Congress (though not designed to frustrate preparations for unconventional war) reinforced the Army's bias toward the European theater.

Second, congressional involvement made presidential choices about how to change the military's mind more difficult. Congressional involvement made controversial personnel decisions politically risky. The most obvious lesson was MacArthur's firing, which, though supported by Congress, presented an opportunity for congressional foes to exact a serious political price from Truman. Thus, presidents tended to choose less risky mechanisms to induce military change. These mechanisms, however, were less likely to result in the change that presidents wanted.

Furthermore, both presidents and military leaders expected that the military could turn to Congress in the event of a disagreement with the president. This changed their strategic calculations, making military leaders more likely to ignore presidential dictates they did not approve of and making presidents wary of pushing the military too hard. Congressional participation in the policy game changed expectations about the political costs and risks of different control strategies.

The American Army's experience in Vietnam does not support the predictions generated by the conventional wisdom on civil-military relations captured by Barry Posen (1984). Posen's model would correctly expect the Army to be resistant to change. However, he would expect presidential intervention to result in military innovation. As we have seen, civilian intervention was unable to force changes in doctrine: presidents proposed innovative doctrine, but the Army maintained its adherence to older, inappropriate doctrine. The Army's resistance to counterinsurgency supports the expectations generated by the institutional model developed in chapter 2. We should expect the Army to innovate only if innovation would help Army leaders pursue their career goals. Because the potential costs

[79] Betts (1977).

of using controversial control of personnel to shape doctrine became too high for presidents to risk, Army leaders paid more attention to congressional control over budgetary allocations.

Even though the containment doctrine required American troops to be flexible to meet a wide variety of threats, incongruities in the interpretation of containment made the preparation for anything outside of the European theater a risky strategy for the Army. This fit well with the reward system in the Army, which emphasized the traditional combat arms.

Because a focus on Europe both served the Army's interest in the competition with the other service branches over the defense budget and reinforced the Army's long-standing bias reflected in its leaders, the budgetary incentives provided little impetus for changing the Army's focus. We should expect, then, that the Army would adapt to the situation in Vietnam only when the changes enhanced its preparation for a war in Europe. As the contrast of the Special Forces and airmobile examples demonstrate, that is precisely what occurred.

# [4]

# *The Central Intelligence Agency and the Marines in Vietnam*

One might argue that the U.S. Army failed to innovate in Vietnam because the task was simply too great—that adaptation to counterinsurgency was too much to ask of U.S. forces. In fact, such adaptation was not too difficult. Service branches with different institutional incentives adapted quickly to the requirements of counterinsurgency doctrine. The CIA and the Marines both created counterinsurgency doctrine well suited for meeting U.S. goals in Vietnam. For somewhat different reasons, individuals in both these organizations had institutional incentives to understand that the communist threat would best be met with a counterinsurgency doctrine—the CIA, because counterinsurgency was close to business as usual and the only military option in which they could participate, and the Marines because their place in the structure of the services had led them to be adaptable.

However, both the relations between the service branches that allowed the Army to take the lead in coordinating the U.S. effort in Vietnam and the Army's methods for evaluating success led the CIA and the Marines to be unlikely organizations for shaping U.S. doctrine in Vietnam. The same budgetary politics that reinforced the Army's emphasis on conventional doctrine weakened those service branches which did not concentrate on the main theaters. In many situations, civilian attempts to garner control over doctrine either were ineffective or inadvertently reinforced the Army's dominance over other branches.

## Success Stories

Both the CIA and the Marines employed a counterinsurgency doctrine during their efforts in Vietnam. These experiences were successful in helping the population resist communist influence. Once the risk of communist terror was reduced, the population was more amenable to the nation-building efforts of the South Vietnamese government, especially at the local level.[1] In addition, the counterinsurgency strategy remedied some of the most pressing problems between American forces and the Vietnamese population. By allowing the American soldiers a chance to know the Vietnamese people at an individual village level, it reduced the amount of general distrust of Vietnamese felt by many American soldiers and gave the servicemen a chance to develop a stake in the conflict.[2] In other words, there is evidence that these episodes of counterinsurgency escaped some of the pressing problems individual servicemen encountered in Vietnam.[3] Also, evidence from the British case and from the American experiments suggests that a counterinsurgency doctrine is easier to sustain over the long term because of its relatively lower cost in men and materials.[4]

Finally, successful counterinsurgency doctrine was not only important for the war against the guerrilla fighters. It was also crucial to stopping the main-force North Vietnamese units in the period before the Tet Offensive. The main-force units depended on the efforts of the local guerrillas to escape U.S. detection. Successful counterinsurgency operations that disrupted these local forces also inhibited the ability of the main-force units to move into position to attack. The overwhelming technical and conventional superiority

---

[1] This amenability, of course, varied according to the skill and honesty of the South Vietnamese government officials.

[2] For examples of this, see West (1985).

[3] For a sampling of analyses on these problems, see Appy (1985), Caputo (1977), Moskos (1970).

[4] Komer (1972), Krulak (1984).

that the U.S. forces held over the communists could best be used in close conjunction with locally based U.S. forces who could direct bombs and artillery toward actual targets and avoid as much as possible the disruption of civilian life.[5]

### The CIA

The CIA's foremost achievement in counterinsurgency was in the development of the CIDG program in the early 1960s.[6] In this program, the CIA used Special Forces detachments in conjunction with CIA case officers and South Vietnamese Special Forces to arm and train Montagnard villagers in the central highlands of Vietnam for self-defense against Vietcong insurgents. The initial experiment was Buon Enao Village in Darlac Province. Members of the U.S. mission approached the Rhade tribal leaders in the fall of 1961 offering them weapons and training in exchange for a declaration of support for the South Vietnamese government and participation in a village self-defense program. The village leaders agreed, and within several months, the program was extended to 40 other Rhade villages. By the end of the summer the program was extended to all of Darlac Province.[7]

Under CIA direction, the Special Forces operated according to classical counterinsurgency doctrine. They worked hand-in-hand with the villagers to fortify village security, build dispensaries, and construct shelters. Early warning systems were set up, and a small number of men were appointed to a strike force. The strike force was a full-time military force that served to patrol the area, set ambushes, and assist villagers under attack. The *village defenders* were also provided with a radio to call for help if their village came under attack. While village forces were being trained at the center in Buon Enao, village security was provided by local security forces. The village self-defense program also provided civic assistance for community development. Service teams were organized to give the villagers training in the use of simple tools, methods of planing, care

---

[5] See Krepinevich (1986), Mangold and Penycate (1986), West (1985).

[6] The CIA had other counterinsurgency efforts (including political action teams) later in the war, which were also successful and were based on a similar philosophy.

[7] Kelly (1973), pp. 24–28.

of crops, and blacksmithing. Village defenders and strike-force medics also conducted clinics. The civic assistance program won widespread popular support.[8]

According to the traditional "oil spot" philosophy, as a cluster of villages became secure, the perimeter was expanded. The system was not limited to Rhade villages but included Vietnamese villages as well. Eventually, new centers similar to Buon Enao were established in five other villages. By August of 1962, the area under the program encompassed two hundred villages. The Buon Enao experiment was a success.[9] The villagers accepted training and weapons enthusiastically and fought well against the Vietcong. Largely due to their efforts, the government declared Darlac Province secure at the end of 1962. Plans were made to turn the program over to the Darlac Province chief and expand to other tribal groups.[10]

### The Marines

Probably the most distinguished story of innovation is that of the CAPs created by the Marines. Under this program by 1970, small groups of Marines were sent to 90 villages in the northern (I Corps) portion of South Vietnam. The Marines would stay in the villages, work with the local militia, get to know the villagers, and use small-scale tactics to disrupt and root out communist infiltration. The patrols used a defensive doctrine: they simply tried to protect a given amount of territory and population from communist activity. This doctrine, however, combined two elements that were essential to successful counterinsurgency in the Vietnam case: (1) it disrupted guerrilla activity, which was essential to the movement of large North Vietnamese forces, and (2) it built trust between the Vietnamese population and the American servicemen. In addition, U.S. Marine units were able to use the sophisticated American communication equipment to call in air support when they encountered

---

[8] Ibid., p. 27.

[9] Not that there were no problems. When General Rosson evaluated the forces, he saw too much emphasis on the strike-force units and offensive action even when the CIA was in charge. Still, the difference between the program under CIA direction and under MACV direction was vast.

[10] Kelly (1973), p. 28.

large North Vietnamese units. This was one of the more appropriate uses of air power in Vietnam.

Because the North Vietnamese forces traveled light and had few logistical resources, they needed access to the local population for food. They depended heavily on the local Vietcong guerrillas both for access to the population and guidance through unknown territory. By disrupting this connection, the CAPs were able to complicate the process of moving large North Vietnamese forces into a position where they could challenge the United States. No village protected by a CAP was repossessed by the Vietcong, and 60 percent of the Marines serving in CAPs volunteered to stay on for an additional six months when they might have returned to the United States.[11]

## REASONS FOR SUCCESS

In sharp contrast with the Army, both the Marines and the CIA responded positively to Kennedy's push for counterinsurgency. Why? Although this is no place for an extensive institutional history of the Marines and the CIA, I shall demonstrate that leaders in the CIA and the Marines expected to be rewarded for adapting to the counterinsurgency challenge. Furthermore, I shall show how past decisions by civilian leaders about how to organize and monitor these institutions led the organizations to reward flexible or adaptable behavior.

### The CIA: Business as Usual

Members of the CIA had two types of incentives to understand the requirements of the counterinsurgency doctrine in Vietnam. First, the CIA was set up to be a flexible institution. From its appropriations arrangement, to its recruitment setup, to its salary scales, the organization was designed to be ad hoc. Perhaps more important, counterinsurgency was the type of military mission for which the CIA prepared. The CIA's general mode of operation was in the range of activities encompassed by a counterinsurgency doc-

[11] Krulak (1984), p. 190.

trine. Thus, individuals in the CIA did not have the same institutional reasons for misunderstanding the situation as did individuals in the Army.

The CIA had its roots in the intelligence office established during World War II.[12] The Office of Strategic Services (OSS) was divided into seven branches, four of which were organized around activities relevant to counterinsurgency doctrine. The Special Operation branch conducted sabotage and worked with resistance forces, the Counterespionage (X-2) branch protected U.S. and Allied intelligence operations from enemy penetration, the Morale Operations branch was responsible for covert propaganda, and the Operational Groups conducted guerrilla operations in enemy territory.[13]

After the war, the Central Intelligence Group (CIG) was established to coordinate and manage military intelligence, so as both to rectify duplications among the military departments and to compensate for any bias their analyses might contain. The National Security Act passed in 1947 changed the CIG to the CIA and reaffirmed its role in intelligence coordination.

The CIA's role in intelligence coordinating prompted backlashes by the military services and the Federal Bureau of Investigation (FBI). The services believed that civilians could not understand (let alone analyze) military information.[14] The FBI was concerned that the CIA would overtaking *its* role in intelligence collection in Latin America.[15] Difficulties with access to military sources of information led the CIA to develop its own information-gathering capabilities. In effect, it became a competing agency in the intelligence picture, rather than a central coordinator.[16]

Within a year of the passage of the National Security Act, the CIA was also charged with the responsibility for covert action. Relations with the Soviet Union had convinced U.S. officials of the need for

---

[12] It was originally established as the Office of Coordinator of Information in the summer of 1941 to collect and analyze information and report directly to the president. A year later, when the United States was embroiled in war with Germany and Japan, the office was renamed the Office of Strategic Services and placed under the direction of the JCS. See Leary (1984), pp. 16–17.

[13] Ibid., p. 17.

[14] Ibid., p. 25.

[15] Ibid., p. 17.

[16] Ibid., pp. 25–27.

an option that offered more than diplomacy but less than war.[17] The CIA, because its OSS component was already familiar with covert action, and its system of unvouchered funds allowed the organization to allocate funds to specific projects without congressional oversight, was a reasonable agency to take on the task.[18]

The covert action mission quickly came to dominate the CIA's attention. Initially, covert action was carried out by the Office of Special Operations (OSO) under the director of central intelligence. Alarm within the government over Soviet activities, however, prompted George Kennan to recommend the creation of a special organization to carry out covert operations.[19] The Office of Policy Coordination (OPC) was formed to undertake the covert action duties. The OPC was paid for within the CIA's appropriations, but its activities were guided by the secretary of state. Policy guidance initially came directly to the OPC director from State and Defense, bypassing the director of central intelligence.[20] For obvious reasons, both the OSO and the director of central intelligence were dissatisfied with this arrangement. The OPC drained funds and prestige away from the CIA. The CIA quickly got the message that rewards were to be gained from covert action, however, and moved its emphasis toward the type of activities undertaken by the OPC.

In 1951, Walter Bedell Smith took over as the director of central intelligence. He directed that orders to the OPC should go through him to the OPC director. Smith then merged the OPC with the OSO to form the Directorate of Plans under Allen Dulles. The merging of the two branches was designed to dampen competition and encourage cooperative action. It also consolidated covert action within the purview of the CIA.

The CIA budget reflects its emphasis on covert action. By 1953,

---

[17] James Forrestal, in particular, was a driving force behind both the concern about the need for a force to counter Soviet covert operations and the emphasis on the CIA as a tool for covert operations. See L. Johnson (1989a), pp. 86–87; Ranelagh (1986), p. 117.

[18] Leary (1984), pp. 24–41. The specific impetus for covert activities was the prospect of communist victory in the 1948 Italian elections. At the inaugural meeting of the NSC in December 1947, a secret annex to Directive NSC 4 (NSC 4A) instructed the director of central intelligence to supplement the State Department propaganda campaign with covert psychological warfare. See Ranelagh (1986), p. 115.

[19] George Kennan was head of the Policy Planning Staff in the State Department.

[20] Leary (1984), p. 42; Ranelagh (1986), pp. 133–134.

the overwhelming majority of CIA resources went to covert operations. While 20 percent of the agency's budget and 40 percent of its personnel were devoted to search, analysis, reporting, and administration, 80 percent of the budget and 60% of the personnel were involved in the Directorate of Plans responsible for covert action.[21] In 1953, Allen Dulles succeeded Smith as the director of central intelligence. In his tenure from 1951 to 1961, Dulles's efforts were almost wholly devoted to covert actions. Dulles did not seize on the numerous technical and analytical developments by the CIA to consolidate—or even strengthen—the agency's position as an intelligence coordinator.[22] Continued resistance by military agencies to CIA coordination of intelligence combined with continued civilian interest in covert action to leave Dulles content with emphasizing the covert action role.[23]

Finally, congressional oversight of the CIA was limited. During the 1950s, there were several attempts by members of Congress to expand their role in oversight of the CIA. The CIA's case that the success of operations demanded a level of secrecy that could not be met with congressional meddling, however, along with strong support for the CIA from interested members of the executive branch and prominent congressmen managed to thwart these efforts.[24] There was also a sense among congressmen in general that given the nature of the CIA's activities, it might be better not to know too much of the intricacies of its operations. In this way, individuals could plead ignorance and not find themselves compromised politically.[25] Congressional decisions not to be actively involved in CIA oversight reduced the possibility that the CIA could use congressional connections to enhance its information collection (as opposed to covert action) role.

Kennedy's call for counterinsurgency drew response form the CIA

---

[21] Ranelagh (1986), p. 202. This figure has fluctuated over time. See L. Johnson (1989a), p. 87.

[22] Leary (1984), p. 72.

[23] Ibid., pp. 72–73. See also Ranelagh (1986), pp. 190–382.

[24] See Leary (1984), pp. 63–67; Ranelagh (1986), pp. 281–85. The congressional efforts did prompt the establishment of a CIA subcommittee of the House Armed Services Committee. But the members of this subcommittee were those who had informally cooperated with the CIA, and there was no formal subcommittee established for appropriations.

[25] Blechman (1990), pp. 138–44.

in part because the structure of delegation and oversight encouraged flexible action by the CIA by keeping Congress out of the relationship. The CIA, had incentives to follow executive instructions to keep from having its action "politicized" by Congress. Also, its accounting procedures gave it the flexibility to respond to presidential directives:[26]

> The CIA was an institution formed in changing times and marked by flexibility.[27]

> the CIA took shape as a "non-bureaucracy." Whether it was developing a new airplane or a new foreign policy, it was to take an innovative, nontraditional approach. . . . Flexibility was the keynote of the CIA.[28]

Even aside from this, counterinsurgency was the mission the CIA had embraced. Adjustment to the situation in Vietnam did not require large innovations. The CIA was able to use the skills it had honed throughout the 1950s to design an appropriate doctrine for Vietnam; and that doctrine in no way threatened the primary mission of the CIA.

## *The Marines: The Adaptable Branch*

Two similar factors induced the Marines to be innovative and adaptable: (1) the unconventional nature of their mission, even in conventional theaters and (2) the insecurity of their mission in theaters dominated by the Army, Navy, and Air Force. These factors

---

[26] This is one of the reasons why Rosson opposed the movement of the CIDG forces from CIA to MACV control. See Rosson (1979), pp. 125–26; Interview with General Williams B. Rosson by Lt. Col. Douglas R. Burgess, William B. Rosson Papers, vol. 2, pp. 229–93, Military History Institute Archives. The ambiguous accounting procedure that gives the CIA flexibility to respond to presidential directives entails risks as well. Without clear accountability rules, the CIA can become carried away with a mission and take action beyond what even the president intends. This difficulty has not been helped by the fact that the president (as well as Congress) wants to be able to claim ignorance about missions that fail. The consequences of these risks have included such bungles as the Bay of Pigs and the Iran/Contra scandal. For an analysis of the difficulties of overseeing the CIA, see Johnson (1988, 1989a, 1989b).

[27] Ranelagh (1986), p. 118.

[28] Ibid., pp. 120–21.

had led the Marines to pride themselves in their adaptability to any challenge and their ability to work on a shoestring:[29]

> In a century and a half, they evolved an elite, almost mystical institutional personality. Partaking variously of pride, aggressiveness, dedication, loyalty, discipline, and courage, this complex personality was— and is—dominated by a conviction that battle is the Marines' only reason for existence and that they must be ready to respond promptly and effectively whenever given an opportunity to fight. Finally, they have come to accept, as an article of faith, that marines must not only be better than everyone else but different as well.[30]

Kennedy's call for counterinsurgency was taken seriously by the Marines, because adaptability to counterinsurgency doctrine was an area in which the Marines had a comparative advantage.

The Marines' position in the U.S. service network was historically tenuous. The Marine force was originally designed as a force to keep sailors from deserting. As improved naval training produced better sailors, Marines became an anachronism, no longer needed to enforce discipline or man the ship's guns. Around the turn of the century, prominent naval thinkers proposed that Marines be removed from the ships and used as expeditionary battalions to support the fleet or U.S. foreign policy abroad. Despite resistance from the Marines, an executive order in November 1908 put this idea into effect. Once they were off the ships, however, Army officers began to pressure for the absorption of Marine forces into the Army. Even as late as the unification debates during and after World War II, the Marines came close to being "merged out of business."[31]

Always an organization on the brink, the Marines were in constant search for a mission that would allow them to maintain their institutional integrity. At the turn of the century this meant playing the role of an expeditionary force, ready for deployment to advanced bases—being the "first to fight." Then, in the interwar period, when

[29] Krulak (1984), chaps. 9–11.
[30] Ibid., p. 3.
[31] See Aldrich (1875), Heinl (1962), Isely and Crowl (1951), Keiser (1982), Krulak (1984), Metcalf (1939), C. Smith (1975). The phrase "merged out of business" comes from Krulak (1984), p. 17.

the Navy's war plan Orange depended on the seizure of defended naval bases, the Marine Corps developed the amphibious assault.[32]

Adaptations by the Marines were often pursued by eager and ambitious innovators over the protests of the conservative officers. Innovators were able to win these battles precisely because they could argue that innovation was needed in order to preserve independent missions for the Marine Corps. For example, the initial interest in amphibious assault was spurned by conservative officers in the Marine Corps, who argued that the corps flourished in direct relation to its distance from the Navy, and that the Marines should continue to focus only on their expeditionary role.[33] Defense reviews in the mid-twenties and early thirties, however, justified the importance of the amphibious assault to an independent role for the Marines, separate enough from Army and Navy missions to justify the continued existence of the Marine Corps.[34] The concern for flexibility and innovation was built into promotion decisions. Officers and enlisted men were rewarded for innovations that worked and often escaped punishment for those that did not.[35] Because Marines were not punished for thinking of new ways to deal with problems even if they went against the book, standard operating procedures for the Marines were often anything but standard.

The National Security Act of 1947 protected the existence of the Marine Corps, but still left its roles and missions subject to the Navy's recommendations. Even Public Law 416 (passed in 1952)—which declared that the U.S. Marine Corps was a separate service acting (along with the U.S. Navy) within the Department of the Navy, ensured a balanced air-and-ground force for the Marines, and provided a seat at the JCS table for the Marines commandant when discussions included the possible use of Marine forces—left the Marine's role in national defense fairly ambiguous.[36] Though the Marines were much less concerned with being disbanded in the post–World War II period, their role in U.S. security was still uncertain enough to keep the organization poised for adaptability.

For these reasons, Kennedy's call for counterinsurgency was taken

[32] Millett (1980), pp. 320–43.
[33] Ibid., p. 322.
[34] Ibid., p. 327–30.
[35] Krulak (1984), pp. 67–69.
[36] Ibid., p. 58.

[86]

seriously by the Marines. Their preparations led them to clash with the MACV in the earliest stages of the conflict. When Marines were first introduced in 1965 to protect the air base at Danang, they argued that the base could not be adequately secured without securing the population around it from communist infiltration. Their first operation of this sort was in the village of Le My, six miles from Danang and heavily infiltrated by communists. A Marine force (two companies) stayed in the village to interdict and root out communist activity. In the process, they assisted the local militia forces to construct defensive positions for the community.[37] The CAPs built on this successful experience.

## THE FAILURE OF COUNTERINSURGENCY

Despite the apparent successes of the counterinsurgency doctrine used by the CIA and the Marines, their efforts never became the central element of U.S. doctrine in Vietnam. The main reason for this had to do with the Army's agenda-setting powers, particularly in measuring success. Once a conflict was large enough for the Army to be involved, it was highly likely that the Army would dominate the planning and implementation of the action. Once the Army was in charge of planning and implementation, it was also in charge of measuring success. In measuring success, the Army emphasized factors important for military victory in line with the theory of war on which it operated. Many of the factors that are important for success in an insurgent war had no place in the Army's list of variables to monitor in Vietnam. Similarly, many of the variables the Army considered most important (e.g., the number of enemy kills) were not exceptionally significant in determining progress in an insurgent war. But because the Army defined the variables it monitored as "military" factors and other variables as something else (often "political" factors) it was difficult to force the Army to broaden its focus. Examining the broader picture would have required the Army to reevaluate its conception of "military."

As it became clear that the terms of the conflict were increasingly set by the Army, both the CIA and the Marines were forced to

---

[37] Ibid., pp. 183–85.

counter the Army on its own turf. The Marines began to argue that their methods killed more communists than the Army, and the CIA argued that the Army's numerical estimates of the enemy were wrong. Similarly, those interested in pacification began to argue that "political," rather than "military," efforts were necessary to pacify the countryside. All these arguments skirted issues that were central for the development of a counterinsurgency doctrine—that kill ratios are not the central goal, that infiltration of the population with informants and the like can be an important part of the war even if it is not a clear "military" action, and that defeat of the enemy requires a political-military effort with the central goal of defending the population from enemy infiltration.

Finally, the institutional mechanisms for overcoming the Army's bias were ineffective. In the Malayan Emergency, as we shall see, delegated control over personnel was a useful mechanism for overcoming resistance to the civil-military effort.[38] Resistant officers were simply removed from power by the high commissioner. The prospect of removal prompted adaptability among middle-range officers who had grown used to World War II formations and plans. In the United States, however, delegated control over personnel was not an option. The best that coordinating structures such as Civilian Operations and Revolutionary Development Support (CORDS) could do was to overlay existing organizational structures: they could not supplant them. Career-minded officers had incentives to pay attention to the requirements of their service branch, rather than the requirements of an ad hoc coordinating agency. This was even true for the MACV, which, as we have seen, did not have very clear control over the Marines' development of the CAP program in the I Corps section of South Vietnam.[39] It was especially true for the CORDS project, where the director was clearly a subordinate member of the MACV structure.

I shall elaborate on these points by examining two cases in depth:

[38] Of course, this doctrine was designed by military leaders. The fact that there were no high-level Army leaders embracing counterinsurgency doctrine had to do with the history of the development of the U.S. Army, and would have made a centralized effort difficult even if the leader had effective control over personnel.

[39] See Luttwak (1985) for an argument that this lack of unity was the main reason for the failure in Vietnam. Much of the defense reform debate in the 1980s revolved around this issue.

the battle between the Army and the CIA over the estimation of enemy forces and the development and implementation of the CORDS project in 1966–67. The former will reveal the difficulty of competing with the Army once the Army had set the terms of the debate; the latter will demonstrate how the relatively low success of the CORDS mission, compared with the British experience in Malaya, can be traced to the greater difficulties with oversight in the U.S. institutional setting.

### The Order-of-Battle Controversy

The order-of-battle controversy between the CIA and the Army provides a good illustration of the way the Army's theories about war and how to define successful war rigged the game against counterinsurgency doctrine. In 1966, the CIA put out a memo, "The Will to Persist," which was based on a lengthy study of the success of American doctrine in Vietnam. The memo argued that the way the war in Vietnam was being fought was unlikely to lead to satisfactory results for the United States.

The memo analyzed the enemy, the type of war the enemy was fighting, and the relevance of U.S. doctrine to that war. It suggested that the Vietnamese communists, learning lessons from their fight against the French, aimed to undermine the American will to persist.[40] The memo speculated that the United States fight to undermine the communists' will to persist was unlikely to work. Bombing was unlikely to result in a reduction in supply below that required to sustain the conflict.[41] And despite reductions in civilian morale, the communist leadership was likely to continue to enjoy the freedom to pursue the conflict in whatever manner it chose.[42] The morale of the communist forces, while seemingly affected by battle hardships, did not have a perceptible impact on their fighting capacity. In fact, incidents of battlefield surrender had gone down.[43] The memo did find that communists were increasingly forced to use armed coercion, rather than persuasion, to maintain the support of

[40] Joint Exhibit No. 217, CBS/Westmoreland Collection, p. 12.
[41] Ibid., Annex I, pp. 7–12.
[42] Ibid., pp. 12–16.
[43] Ibid., Annex VI, pp. 1–8.

the rural population, which was crucial to their supplies of food and the mobility of their main forces.[44] This suggested that measures to protect the rural population might yield useful results.

The CIA, however, chose to fight the MACV not over the inappropriateness of the Army's military doctrine, but over the Army's misestimation of communist irregular forces in the order of battle. The CIA chose to fight about "hard numbers," rather than elusive theories of war, because it was unlikely to win a battle about war with the Army. By focusing on the battle it could win, rather than the battle that mattered, however, the CIA ended up losing both contests. It was unable to get the Army to take counterinsurgency more seriously.

Order-of-battle estimates are an important part of any commander's information. They provide estimates of the number of forces that are likely to be faced in battle and keep track of specific enemy units, their movements, and so on, which are helpful in planning attacks and predicting the enemy's behavior. In Vietnam, the Army's plans for defeating the communist threat in Southeast Asia came to be based on an attrition doctrine. Although U.S. objectives were defined much more broadly, the MACV saw its particular role as killing enemy forces to the point that the enemy would no longer be able to supply men for the field.[45] As put in 1966, the fundamental objective for American forces was to "attrit, by year's end, VC/NVA forces at a rate as high as their capacity to put men into the field."[46] According to Maxwell Taylor:

> The basic limit [to the U.S. deployments] is the willingness of Hanoi to continue the aggression in spite of the mounting costs. Just at what point they will decide this is not a remunerative course of action I just do not know. But they are the ones really to decide what the limit will be. . . .

[44] Ibid., Annex III, pp. 1–20.

[45] As this and the next section will make clear, other tasks (defense, pacification, etc.) were delegated to other forces, particularly the Army of the Republic of Vietnam.

[46] See "1966 Program To Increase the Effectiveness of Military Operations and Anticipated Results Thereof," drafted by Bill Bundy and John McNaughton, Joint Exhibit No. 215D, *Westmoreland v. Columbia Broadcasting System*, p. 2, CBS/Westmoreland Collection. This document lists five other results, four of which concentrate on defensive and pacification measures, and one that concentrates on VC/NVA base destruction. The Army's position from the summer of 1965 had been that its role in the overall

If we could continue the rate [of loss of guerrillas] which has been going on in 1966, theoretically they would virtually run out of trained troops by the end of 1966.[47]

The attrition doctrine and its infamous "crossover point"[48] also caused the order-of-battle estimates in Vietnam to be an exceedingly important part of the Army's *measure of success*. Order-of-battle estimates—which summarized the results of the body count, estimates of North Vietnamese Army (NVA) infiltration, Vietcong recruitment, and the status of specific enemy units—were used to measure progress toward achieving the attrition objective.

The MACV analysts monitored four types of enemy units to develop the order-of-battle estimates: NVA forces and Vietcong main, local and irregular forces (including guerrilla, self-defense, and secret self-defense forces).[49] In general, the military analysts had much greater confidence in their estimation of enemy *main* forces because their organization along conventional military lines made them easier to monitor. The duties of the irregular forces were less clear and more difficult to judge.[50] The MACV analysts readily admitted that their focus was on the "primary threat" (the enemy's hard-core forces) and that they were "forced to rely on broad estimates for the other categories."[51] However, even in the hard-core categories, there

---

strategy was to find and kill main-force units. The less glamorous pacification tasks were left to ARVN. See Krepinevich (1986), pp. 164–68.

[47] Maxwell Taylor's testimony to the Senate Foreign relations committee, from U.S., Congress, Senate, Committee on Foreign Relations, *To Amend Further the Foreign Assistance Act of 1961 as Amended (Vietnam Hearings)*, 89th Cong. 2d sess., 1966, p. 524, quoted in Palmer (1978), p. 79.

[48] The point at which the United States would begin to win because they were able to kill the enemy faster than he could supply new forces.

[49] North Vietnamese Army units were trained in North Vietnam and composed of mostly North Vietnamese; the Vietcong main forces were directly subordinate to the Central Office for South Vietnam (COSVN); Vietcong local forces normally only operated within a given province or district and were subordinate to provincial or district party committees; and irregular forces operated at the hamlet or village level to provide a wide array of support for Vietcong activities. See USMACV Ac of S J-2, PERINTREP [Periodic Intelligence Report], February 1967, pp. vi–vii.

[50] See discussion in Pacific Command, "Report of the Conference To Standardize Methods for Developing and Presenting Statistics on OB Infiltration and Estimates," 21 Feb. 1967; Joint Exhibit No. 227 CBS/Westmoreland Collection.

[51] MACV Briefing on the Enemy Order of Battle, 24 Nov. 1967, Joint Exhibit No. 277, CBS/Westmoreland Collection.

were some problems. The conservative methodology for estimating enemy infiltration led to long delays in counting new enemy personnel, while enemy casualties were quickly deducted from the order of battle.[52] This produced a skewed estimate.

The primary point of contention between the MACV and the CIA, however, was in the estimation of irregular forces. In mid-1966, MACV analysts evinced concern when captured documents indicated that the irregular forces numbers in the order of battle were too low.[53] A CIA working paper followed up on this concern and supported it.[54] After receiving a copy of the CIA paper, the order-of-battle component of the MACV sent an intelligence collection requirement to all provinces in South Vietnam, asking them to review their irregular holdings according to CIA methodology.[55] Using the new methodology, the report for one province (Quang Tin) estimated 17,027 irregulars, in dramatic contrast with the previous MACV holding of 1,700 irregulars.[56]

Almost simultaneous with the initial MACV analysts' concern about low estimates came the CIA memo, "The Will to Persist."[57] While the memo acknowledged the disputes over the estimates of irregular forces, its pessimistic perspective on the potential for U.S. success with an attrition strategy was validated without any increase in the estimates of irregular forces. There is certainly a connection between the CIA's better understanding of the type of war the United States was fighting and the seriousness with which it regarded irregular forces. There is also a connection between the Army's refusal to take the irregular forces seriously and its focus on an attrition strategy. But the connection between better estimates of

[52] The MACV's methodology required that at least two captured documents and/or two prisoner interrogation reports had to confirm the existence of a unit before it was added to the order of battle.

[53] Memo, B. F. Layton to A. Smith, 16 Aug. 1966, Joint Exhibit No. 277, CBS/Westmoreland Collection.

[54] "The Strength of the Viet Cong Irregulars" (CIA Working Paper), referred to in Joint Exhibit No. 219 (Memo, Samuel Adams to Chief, Indochina Division, 7 Nov. 1966), CBS/Westmoreland Collection.

[55] CIA methodology both required less stringent verification procedures and added other categories, specifically, "Assault Youth."

[56] Memo, Adams to Chief, Indochina Division, 7 Nov. 1966, Joint Exhibit No. 219, CBS/Westmoreland Collection.

[57] "The Will to Persist" (CIA Memo), 26 Aug. 1966, Joint Exhibit No. 217, CBS/Westmoreland Collection.

irregular forces and a change in Army doctrine is not clear. By fighting the Army over the estimation of enemy forces, the CIA analysts were distracted from the more important battle over appropriate doctrine.

The battle over appropriate doctrine, however, was not likely to be taken seriously by the MACV. The Army could say (as it had all along) that civilians simply do not understand military matters. By focusing on hard numbers, the CIA analysts could force the military to taking them seriously. As in the "drunkard's search," the CIA chose to fight the battle it could win, rather than the battle that mattered.[58] The CIA's institutional position left them without a winning strategy for forcing the Army to take counterinsurgency more seriously.

As it was, the group of CIA analysts led by Samuel Adams, put increasing pressure on the CIA leadership to force the MACV to change its methodology and to include new categories of irregulars (assault youths) in the order of battle. The MACV and its Defense Intelligence Agency (DIA) argued that because the irregular forces were the least important and the hardest to estimate and because an increase in the (unimportant) estimates would be devastating to American public opinion, it would be foolish to change the estimates. The battle continued until the fall of 1967, when an intelligence conference was held to resolve the dispute. Conversations at this conference led Samuel Adams to accuse Westmoreland and the upper echelons of the military bureaucracy of a conspiracy to keep the estimation of enemy forces under three hundred thousand and to link the overly rosy estimations to the surprise of the Tet Offensive in early 1968.[59]

Unfortunately, as with the drunk searching for his keys in the light rather than where he dropped them, the CIA could not win the battle over force numbers without also arguing that the impor-

---

[58] The "drunkard's search" is a story in which a drunk looks for his keys under a street light even though he dropped them near the car. When asked why he doesn't look closer to where he dropped the keys, he replies that he can't see in the dark. See Popkin (1991), pp. 74, 92–94. To give the CIA some credit, however, we must note that there was a connection, however vague, between taking irregulars seriously and fighting a different type of war. This connection was lost as Samuel Adams went on a crusade to correct what he saw as an Army conspiracy to deceive.

[59] For different sides of this debate, see Adams (1975), McGarvey (1970), Wirtz (1990).

tance of the irregular forces brought the Army's doctrine into question. Certainly, the CIA did not want the MACV to kill all the people it wanted them to include in the order of battle. As Renata Adler rather unceremoniously pointed out, if those people included in the order of battle were simply new targets, incidents like My Lai are seen in a new light.[60] Part of what the CIA sought to make the Army understand was that when children and grandparents are participating in an insurgent effort, the nature of the war is different and so is the doctrine most likely to win.[61] In the event, the numbers-battle lost these subtleties. Once the Army had set the terms of the debate over success, the likelihood of the CIA's winning a meaningful battle over doctrine was lost.

## CORDS *and the Failure to Set Up an Adaptation Process*

After ten years of civilian attempts to get the Army to develop a counterinsurgency doctrine for Vietnam, the best results came from a structure that separated pacification from military activities and placed the pacification effort within the MACV structure. CORDS both took pacification seriously and succeeded in garnering relatively more resources from the Army once it was situated within the MACV structure. However, the pacification effort still remained an adjunct to the real war, and it was never able seriously to affect the course of Army doctrine. Only when the war had changed, after the Tet Offensive, did the CORDS program register its modest successes.

Although efforts to move the Army toward a counterinsurgency doctrine continued in the 1962–67 period, without a coordinating force, they drifted aimlessly.[62] As a *Pentagon Papers* analyst noticed, a major problem with the implementation of a pacification program was that neither the United States nor the Government of Vietnam (GVN) had an adequate plan, program, or management structure for dealing with pacification. The combination of the MACV/JCS preoccupation with the "real war" and the lack of a unified civil-

---

[60] Adler (1986a), p. 60.

[61] Some in the CIA—and Adams in particular—also wanted to argue that given the nature of the war, the United States should not be involved.

[62] Blaufarb (1977), pp. 205–23; Komer (1972).

military direction in either the GVN or the United States hindered the construction of such a plan.[63]

The first concerted effort to integrate pacification efforts was initiated in 1966 with the CORDS program. The CORDS program, however, did not have the requisite features to impose pacification goals on the Army. At best, it was a separate coordinating force of the civilian efforts. Eventually, it became a coordinating mechanism under MACV command. No CORDS official, however, ever had any authority over Army operations or the judgment as to Army success rates. There was also a general assumption that pacification was an exercise to be done after the main-force requirements were met: in other words, pacification was part of mopping up. There was little sense of the importance of counterinsurgency for meeting the requirements of fighting the North Vietnamese main-force units.[64]

To the degree that the Army endorsed pacification activities, it endorsed the use of Army of the Republic of Vietnam (ARVN) to support revolutionary development—this despite the fact that the United States had trained the ARVN as an offensive force: "Since its inception, ARVN has been oriented, trained and led toward the task of offensive operations. . . . It is difficult, in a short period of time, to redirect the motivation and training of years, *and to offset the long indoctrination that offensive action against the VC is the reason for the existence of the Army.*"[65] Many rationales were given for this prescription despite much evidence that the ARVN was not prepared for this task. Most prominent was the supposition that Vietnam would be worse off if it came to rely upon U.S. forces. United States forces would (eventually) go home, and the area would fall again. Of course, the experiences of the CIA and the Marines suggest differently. There, the close operations of the American troops with the local security forces *enhanced* the ability of these local forces to maintain their security even after the U.S. forces had left.[66]

More important, eradicating the communist threat did not equal clearing an area of main-forces units. The experience of the Marines, particularly, demonstrates the close relationship between pacifica-

---

[63] *Pentagon Papers* (1971–72), vol. 2, pp. 573–74.
[64] Ibid., p. 548.
[65] Ibid., p. 587.
[66] See Peterson (1989), West (1985).

tion activities and main-force operations. In order to clear an area of main-force threats, the U.S. forces needed to do more than simply sweep through. United States forces participating in pacifying an area could play an important part in disrupting the potential for future main-force activity, which was crucial for eradicating the communist threat. The setup of communications and reliable and timely responses to communist movements was crucial to local security. If some U.S. forces were participating in a pacification project, the likelihood of reliable responses to communist movements was much higher than if only the ARVN was supplying support. This was true in part because of the relative quality of the forces and in part because of the greater response of U.S. firepower to threatened U.S. forces.

The structure of the CORDS program also reflects the separation between political and military tasks that the Army endorsed. The assumption behind the CORDS program was that civil-military integration was necessary in the sense that some force was needed to hold an area after the Army had eradicated main-force communist troops. There was little room in this conception for the type of operations in which the Marines or the CIA had been involved. In fact, the Army thought it would be better if the U.S. troops had as little contact with the local population as possible. To the degree that local Vietnamese forces needed military support, it was determined that the ARVN should provide that support.[67] The 1967 plan assigned to the ARVN the primary task of supporting pacification and to the U.S. forces the task of destroying Vietcong/NVA main forces and base areas.[68] Unfortunately, however, these were not separable activities.

Even so, in late 1966, Washington undertook its most significant effort to coordinate the civilian agencies involved in pacification. The initial reorganization created the Office of Civilian Operations (OCO) as a coordinating agency separate from the MACV. It was clear from the beginning that this separation was dependent on

---

[67] Interestingly, the Army's interest in separating itself from the Vietnamese population fed into civilian concerns about nation building and the proper role for an outside power. Thus, by the mid-sixties, assumptions about the importance of using Vietnamese forces for pacification had crept into civilian analyses as well as military ones.

[68] *Pentagon Papers* (1971–72), vol. 2, p. 587.

fairly dramatic and immediate evidence of success. Dramatic evidence of success was not immediately forthcoming, and the OCO structure was (again) revised and placed under MACV command as a mechanism for coordinating civilian efforts from within the MACV. This launched the CORDS program.

By bringing the CORDS program within the MACV structure, the United States, for the first time since its initial commitment in Vietnam, operated within a single structure of authority. This, as we will see from the Malayan case, was a promising step for the development of a counterinsurgency doctrine. It was also a crucial step for moving the requisite resources to pacification. According to Robert Komer: "My view was a very simple one: if you are ever going to get a program going, you are only going to be able to do it by stealing from the military. They have all the trucks, they have all the planes, they have all the people, they have all the money—and what they did not have locked up, they had a lien on."[69] By introducing a new organization created entirely around the mission of pacification and placing its pacification effort within the MACV structure, the development of CORDS resulted in greater U.S. civilian influence over pacification than had ever existed in Vietnam. It also allowed pacification efforts to have a greater claim on military resources (both U.S. and GVN).[70]

All in all, however, the CORDS project had relatively little influence on the Army's activities. In exchange for the Army's support for the CORDS concept, McNamara did not push too hard for direct Army troop involvement in pacification, and Komer did not interfere with the large search-and-destroy operations the MACV was drawing up for 1967 and beyond.[71] The Army could deflect State Department criticism about its war of attrition by pointing to its new commitment to pacification, without great cost to its doctrine.

Civilian leaders' inability to delegate the power over personnel to any central organization meant that the ad hoc organization's goals were competing with long-standing agency goals. To the extent that these goals were in conflict, individuals interested in their careers

---

[69] Thompson and Frizzell (1977), p. 191.
[70] Komer (1972), p. 114.
[71] Krepinevich (1986), pp. 217–18.

were likely to pay attention to their agency, rather than the ad hoc organization.[72]

Incidentally, the lack of central control affected not only the ability of the civilian leadership to force the military to think about counter-insurgency but also the degree to which any organization was able to run the show. For example, the Marines ran their operation in the I Corps area in significant opposition to the MACV's concept.[73] This was a problem encountered throughout the CORDS effort. It was clear that the structure of incentives continued to encourage individuals to pay attention to their particular agency, rather than to any central command.[74] This contrasts sharply with the experience of the British in Malaya. There, delegated control over personnel allowed the central commander in Malaya to operate outside the jurisdiction of any particular agency in order to create an integrated and concerted effort.

Unfortunately, we do not have a clear test of the effectiveness of the CORDS concept. It had most of its effect after the 1968 Tet Offensive, which radically changed the nature of the conflict in Vietnam by both increasing popular support for the GVN (as the alternative to the Vietcong) and destroying the Vietcong infrastructure, which had provided crucial support for the North Vietnamese and Vietcong main-force units.[75]

## The Electoral Structure and Civilian Advice

Much of the literature on the Vietnam War puts heavy blame on civilian leaders (mostly presidents) too concerned with electoral politics to do the job that was required in Vietnam. I have argued that if we expect presidents to make policy choices that will hurt them electorally, we will often be disappointed. *Of course* presidents will pay attention to electoral concerns. In incidences of divided

---

[72] The implications of individual agency goals on policy is discussed in Komer (1972).

[73] *Pentagon Papers* (1971–72), vol. 2, p. 534. See Luttwak (1985) for a critique of the U.S. experience in Vietnam from this perspective.

[74] *Pentagon Papers* (1971–72), vol. 2, p. 537.

[75] See Pond (1972) on the changes after Tet.

government, I have argued, this will often lead presidents to be reluctant to control military doctrine by replacing military leaders.[76]

Electoral concerns can also lead presidents to make contradictory demands on a military, which helps to undermine their ability to direct military doctrine. When faced with conflicting demands, the military organization can choose the demand it can most easily fulfill. This was part of the Johnson administration's problem in getting the Army to pay attention to pacification. The administration wanted *fast counterinsurgency:* many would argue this was a self-contradictory demand.[77] The administration's concern with speed helped to undermine its pressure for a realistic counterinsurgency policy.

Also, Robert McNamara's belief that the military effort could be judged by quantifiable indicators undoubtedly added to the difficulties of getting a serious counterinsurgency effort going. It is difficult to quantify counterinsurgency success.[78] Dead bodies, however, were easy to quantify and provided a clear (if largely irrelevant) indicator of success. The Army's use of body counts satisfied the quantification criterion.[79]

Thus, the way civilians decided to monitor the military affected the variables to which the military paid attention. Civilian leaders told the Army to adapt to counterinsurgency but monitored variables that were either easy to observe (body counts) or had to do with other factors than the change to counterinsurgency (speed). The Army was effectively resistant to the ideas of counterinsurgency even during Kennedy's reign, when the president was more adept at monitoring change. The confused signals sent at the beginning of the war by the Johnson administration enhanced the Army's re-

---

[76] Even after 1964, when Johnson faced a friendly Congress (democratically controlled, at least), the political consequences of removing military personnel during a conflict were not lost. After all, Truman had congressional support when he replaced MacArthur, but he still suffered politically.

[77] See Krulak (1984), p. 186.

[78] The United States certainly tried. Pacification was eventually judged by a Hamlet Evaluation System (HES) indicator. See Komer (1986), Thompson and Frizzell (1977).

[79] McNamara has claimed that he could use the statistics to see through the MACV's strategy (Shapley 1993, pp. 150–61). On the other hand, he testified that although the body count was a terrible thing, "if you're secretary of defense and you're concerned about whether you are progressing militarily and it is said to be a, quote, 'war of attrition,' unquote, . . . then it is important to try to understand whether you are accomplishing the attrition or not" (quoted in Shapley 1993, pp. 251–52).

sistance. Because the Army could calculate success on an indicator that civilian leaders could also monitor—body counts—and that also promised quick success, the Army was not automatically threatened by other service branches' adaptations in counterinsurgency doctrine.

I have shown that adaptation to counterinsurgency was not too difficult for U.S. forces. The CIA and the Marines, both with appropriate institutional incentives, adapted quickly to the requirements of insurgent warfare and created a counterinsurgency doctrine that was appropriate to the situation in Vietnam. Why, then, did civilian leaders not reward the innovative service branches with a more central role in implementing U.S. policy in Vietnam? The civilian institutional arrangement impeded this type of solution. Replacing personnel to change doctrine was a politically risky strategy for presidents. For political reasons, presidents were unwilling even to delegate control over personnel in order to standardize doctrine under the MACV structure, let alone to change doctrine by putting a Marine in charge. This, as we shall see, contrasts sharply with the British in Malaya.

The problem was further complicated by the fact that the Army's privileged position in the service hierarchy with respect to land actions assured the Army a leading agenda-setting role in any large action. Once the Army set the terms for competition, it became difficult for civilian leaders even to evaluate the successes of other service branches. By the Army's measures, it was successful in Vietnam. Hardly an expert in military matters, President Johnson could scarcely judge which measure of success was most important.[80]

The Army's argument against the doctrine pursued by the CIA and the Marines was that it was political, not military. CIA documents calling the Army's theory of success into question were dismissed as not properly focusing on the military element. CIA personnel then chose to contest the Army's success on the Army's own terms, because such a criticism would have to be taken seri-

---

[80] This difficulty was further enhanced by the other questions surrounding the conflict with Vietnam. Primarily, in the early years, these questions focused on the risk of escalation. But after the war had "dragged on" for a couple of years, there were also nagging doubts about whether the United States should even be in Vietnam. These issues prevented a clear focus on doctrine as the crucial question.

ously. The ensuing controversy over the order of battle and the estimates of enemy forces did get the Army's attention. Without being tied to an argument about doctrine, however, the numbers-battle had little effect on doctrine. Similarly, the advocates of pacification achieved their greatest success when they agreed to contain their operations within the political realm. The CORDS structure succeeded bureaucratically because it operated within the MACV's military structure without questioning the Army's military operations.

Finally, we must allocate appropriate blame to civilian leaders within the administrations. Especially in the Johnson administration, civilian attempts to micromanage military operations often fed into the Army's resistance. It was easier for the Army to resist the importance of the Marine experiments in the CAP program because they could point to civilian leaders' concern with speed and argue that the CAP concept was simply too slow. Also, McNamara's obsession with quantifying success increased the attraction of body counts as a measure of success.

It must be noted, however, that the importance of civilian expertise at micromanagement is relevant because of the structure of civilian institutions. As the British cases will show, civilian expertise in micromanagement is less important for successful adaptation when military organizations are biased toward adaptability or when civilian leaders can freely use control over personnel to change doctrine.

# [5]

## *The Boer War and Malaya:*
## *Why the British Army Adapted*

In both the Boer War and Malaya, British military leaders adjusted doctrine to meet peripheral threats. They thereby ensured that military doctrine would be integrated with British grand strategy. In the Boer War, this was a formidable task. In Malaya, the task that faced the British military was even more difficult. The jungle terrain, the prior orientation of the Army for large-scale war in Europe, and the complexities of nation building as a political goal made the Malayan Emergency a formidable problem. These factors also made the British Army's task in the Malayan Emergency a closer approximation to the task the United States faced in Vietnam.

This chapter demonstrates that the integration of British military doctrine in the Boer War with Britain's grand strategy was not the result of civilian intervention. In fact, civilian leaders were generally uninterested in military doctrine.[1] Instead, I establish that military doctrine was integrated with grand strategy because unified civilian control had allowed civilian leaders in Britain to bias the Army toward paying attention to their goals. Because Army officers expected to be rewarded for adapting, they adapted. As I argued in Chapter 3, the unification of the civilian leadership in Parliament and the Cabinet allowed political leaders to use control over personnel with-

---

[1] The one civilian leader who was concerned with doctrine, Lord Milner, the high commissioner of South Africa, was unable to force the Army to pursue the doctrine he thought was appropriate. Instead, different Army leaders pursued their own form of innovative doctrine against the Boers.

out running political risks. The ease with which civilians could use control over personnel affected the character of the professionalized Army in Britain. The education and promotion structure reflected the wide variety of missions that the British Army undertook, rather than the narrow goals of military science.[2] In addition, the prospect of losing one's job if the Army failed to accomplish its task made military leaders more sensitive to political goals. Unified civilian leadership eased oversight problems for civilian leaders in Britain by making personnel decisions an effective tool for altering the preference structure of the Army.

The British Army's behavior in the Malayan Emergency was more closely connected to civilian intervention. In particular, civilian leaders (acting on military advice) delegated authority over promotions to the field commander to ensure that military personnel were rewarded for adaptive behavior. These steps were likely because the unified institutional structure in Britain allowed politicians to use personnel policy to induce adaptation without fear of electoral retribution.

These cases do not imply that doctrine will always be perfectly integrated in countries with unified civilian leadership: during the Boer War, military leaders anticipated civilian leaders' goals for adaptable doctrine but not the electorate's goals for humane doctrine. Nor do they imply that there is no agency loss: the more civilian leaders pay attention to military results and changes in the international order, the more encouraged military leaders will be to anticipate their preferences. However, the more civilian leaders' concerns with short-term political goals are divorced from long-term security goals, the more we might expect military leaders also to be worried about short-term goals.[3] We might then see something like what Samuel Huntington calls "subjective civilian control."[4]

---

[2] Undoubtedly, the variety of tasks the British Army was called upon to perform in the defense of the empire had a positive effect on the adaptability of the Army. Nonetheless, this is not a sufficient condition for adaptability. The U.S. Army, too, was called upon to do a wide variety of tasks in the nineteenth century; but it was still able to instill the values of military science in its organization. The British Army was not. We must look beyond the mission of the organizations to explain this variation.

[3] Friedberg (1988) has blamed political motivations for civilian leaders' failure to adjust British grand strategy realistically at the turn of the century.

[4] See Huntington (1957).

One could attribute the lack of preparation for the Boer War to precisely this.

Also, domestic political struggles were echoed in military appointments. As we shall see, the replacement of General Sir Redvers Buller with General Lord Roberts owed as much to shady political oneupmanship as it did to Buller's initial failures. In addition, the civil-military structure before the Boer War was not very effective at creating institutional coherence or an institutional memory.[5] Often, individual military leaders innovated in different ways to the same threat. During the Boer War, different campaigns were fought in entirely different ways.

As Chapter 2 has demonstrated, after the Boer War, the British Army instituted structural reforms to create greater institutional coherence. The resulting process encouraged a military professionalism sensitive to long-term civilian goals. Some have argued that this process produced a diluted form of professionalism: "The British Army is not an institution able to express views and to propose decisions on professional grounds alone."[6] The way in which consistent, politically motivated civilian oversight affected the professionalization of the military in Britain ensured that doctrine would be closely coordinated with political policy.

## MILITARY DOCTRINE IN SOUTH AFRICA

The events leading up the Boer War look quite different from those leading up to the U.S. intervention in Vietnam. Civilian leaders did not systematically try to change military doctrine in the period preceding the Boer War. In fact, concern with the budget and the possibility for political negotiations kept civilian leaders from noticing or acting upon war preparations by the Boers. As the war began, however, the military quickly recognized its losses and adapted to the circumstances in South Africa.

### The Background

The turn-of-the-century conflict between the British and the Boers had its roots in an earlier struggle. The Boers, surrounded by hostile

[5] Bidwell and Graham (1982).
[6] Ibid., p. 294.

Bantu tribes in 1877, acquiesced in a British decision to annex and protect them. Within a few years, however, a number of Boer leaders took steps to regain independence. Their rebellion was met by both negotiations and British troops under the command of General George Colley. When a surprise attack by the Boers killed Colley and drove off his troops, the British acted to settle the matter immediately and granted autonomy to the Boers with a few strings attached—British suzerainty, some restraints on external treaty making, and vague guarantees for the citizen rights of European residents.[7] Conflict over these strings—particularly the voting rights of British immigrants (Uitlanders)—resulted in the outbreak of war in 1899.

The first shock that the British encountered in South Africa was that the Boers were equipped with modern, superior weaponry that overpowered old-fashioned British weapons and tactics. The charge was ineffective against machine guns. The first adaptations that Great Britain made were modernizing ones. To the degree that these adaptations were heeded after the war, they led Britain toward a doctrine that would be more successful in a modern war against other major powers.[8]

Within a year, the British cavalry carried rapid-firing rifles in the place of lances, used artillery for the defensive, had innovated in the use of machine guns, and had captured the capitals of the Transvaal and the Orange Free State. The collapse of the capitals, however, did not involve a surrender by Boer military leaders. Instead, the Boers launched a series of guerrilla attacks, which, in the end, proved much more difficult for the British to adapt to. General Roberts left South Africa to General Lord Kitchener for "mopping up" operations in the fall of 1900 less than one year after he took the reins from a battered General Buller. Kitchener would not leave for eighteen more months.

British military doctrine in the Boer War was not perfect. In fact, the initial advances made by the Boers were a blow to both the British imperial self-image and to the world's image of British power. Most histories of the Boer War treat it as a black moment in British

[7] Selby (1970), p. 190.

[8] Jay Stone (1985) makes the argument that the British lessons learned in South Africa were responsible for the success of British intervention, which prevented the Schlieffen plan from working.

history. Nonetheless, the Army's ability to realize its initial losses and change its approach to the war in order effectively to counter the Boers must be regarded as a successful case of adaptation.

## Civilian Disregard and Military Adaptation

The Intelligence Office had noted an increase in war provisions, including armament shipments into South Africa as early as 1896. Under Ardagh, both preparations by the Boers and the difficulties and requirements of a campaign against them were reported. At least seven reports were submitted to the commander in chief. All of these were informally discussed with Secretary of State for War Lansdowne.[9] The earliest dispatches advised serious consideration of the possibility of a Boer invasion of Natal. A September 1898 memorandum pointed out "the Transvaal has, during the last two years, made military preparations on a scale which can only be intended to meet the contingency of a contest with Great Britain".[10]

As late as September 6, 1899, however, memos and letters between Chief of Staff Viscount Wolseley, Secretary of State for War Lansdowne, and Colonial Secretary Joseph Chamberlain demonstrate a conviction on the part of Lansdowne and Chamberlain that the intelligence reports exaggerated the size of the Boer force.[11] Both Commander in Chief Wolseley and Sir Alfred Milner (high commissioner for South Africa and lieutenant governor of Cape Colony) thought that the British forces in position were much too small to protect the security of the British colonies. Milner proposed that Great Britain send an overwhelming force of 10,000 men to South Africa. Wolseley's recommendation was that they should mobilize all of Sir Redvers Buller's (commander in chief for South Africa) First Army

[9] Henry Charles Keith "Clan" Petty-Fitzmaurice, fifth marquess of Lansdowne.

[10] Hamer summarizes the Report of the Royal Commission on the War in South Africa (1970), p. 202.

[11] Fergusson (1984), pp. 113–14. Although it would not have been surprising if the reports were off (the intelligence department was notoriously understaffed and underfunded, so much so that it did not even have maps of the Natal area), the Report of the Royal Commission on the War in South Africa found that the reports were very close to accurate. (Ardagh estimated that the Boers would put a maximum of 48,000 men in arms, and the actual numbers at the end of the war were reckoned to be some 12,000 more than that.) See Symons (1963), p. 64. These numbers are roughly corroborated in Fergusson, p. 114.

and a cavalry division (a total of 35,000 men) in a demonstration of Britain's might to Paul Kruger.[12] These proposals were scoffed at for their extravagance by Secretary of State for War Lansdowne.

At the level of prime minister, Lord Salisbury was chiefly concerned with the effect of the South African problem on British relations with Germany.[13] He was also worried about the difficulties of mobilizing the population behind a war with South Africa. "We cannot afford to have more than a limited area of heather alight at one time," he warned Joseph Chamberlain (colonial minister).[14] In addition, it was feared that war preparations might aggravate the Boers and prevent a peaceful settlement.[15] Through the summer, British civilian leadership continued to hope that a conflict with the Boers could be avoided. The urges to mobilize as tensions mounted in early 1899 were resisted for fear of ruining a political solution.[16] The wisdom of this policy was reinforced by a concern with spending, and both served to bolster the skepticism with which politicians viewed intelligence reports on Boer mobilization.

A report in late spring that it would take as much as four months to mobilize the British forces for South Africa shocked the government. If hostilities should break out, it was feared that Britain could not get her troops there on time. To ensure the security of the colonies in the short run, Commander Sir George White and 10,000 troops from India were dispatched to South Africa in June. When the war began in October, the British fielded a force only about one-half the size of the Boer force.[17]

The greatest British setbacks, however, were not recorded until *after* the full force of the regular British military was physically present in South Africa. In early December, the defeats during "Black Week" left the army, the government, and the public reeling. Reserves were called up (from both Britain and the colonies) and Sir

---

[12] Packenham (1979), pp. 66–68. Buller had been appointed commander in chief after the failure of the Bloemfontein Conference in June 1899. Kruger was the president of the Transvaal, Steyn was the president of the Orange Free State. Both Boer republics participated in the war.

[13] Balfour (1985), p. 235.

[14] Ibid., p. 240.

[15] Barnett (1970), p. 338.

[16] This is an example of what Robert Jervis (1976) calls a security dilemma.

[17] There were roughly 20–27 thousand British soldiers against 47–57 thousand Boer soldiers and volunteers. See Balfour (1985), p. 260.

Redvers Buller was replaced as commander in chief by Lord Roberts. Common knowledge has it that Buller's supposed contemplation of the surrender of Ladysmith prompted the decision to supersede him with Roberts. The dynamics of this decision are interesting, however, in what they show us about civil-military relations in Britain.

I have argued that political control over the military was effective, in part, because civilians could use control over military personnel without fears of political retribution. The removal of Buller demonstrates this claim. It was politicians who made the decision to remove Buller from command. The commander in chief found out about the decision after it went into effect. Unlike Truman's removal of MacArthur, this choice had very few political consequences. This contrast is especially striking because the choice of Roberts to replace Buller involved substantial rivalries between factions of the Army and politicians in the Cabinet.

In many ways, Roberts was the obvious choice as the next senior officer. He was the head, however, of what was called the Roberts Ring, or the "Indians," which was pitted against the Wolseley Ring, or the "Africans." The Wolseley Ring had dominated promotion mechanisms for years as an informal patronage network. Wolseley had been the right-hand man of the duke of Cambridge when he was commander in chief, and then was appointed to replace him. The Roberts Ring had no patronage of its own. It was formed of those officers who had been denied Wolseley's patronage.

Buller was Wolseley's protégé. Secretary of State Lansdowne, who had been viceroy of India, and worked closely with Roberts, had pushed for Roberts's appointment in South Africa. This was initially resisted by the prime minister, Lord Salisbury out of personal distrust for Roberts. After Buller's famous telegram, however, the prime minister agreed to the change.[18] Despite the fact that Buller's replacement was a pretty shady political deal, there were no political consequences to Lord Salisbury's decision. There was no effective alternative civilian institution to which dissatisfied Army officers could appeal.

As it turns out, British intelligence reports had focused on the

---

[18] Packenham (1979), pp. 252–64.

shortage of mere numbers of British troops and weapons. They were much less astute to the problems of comparing the relative strengths of British versus Boer soldiers (i.e., differences in support requirements and mobility).[19] These factors were to play a large role in British difficulties even before the Boers turned to guerrilla tactics. The initial encounters between the British and the Boers demonstrated a host of problems with British doctrine.

First, the British relied entirely on the railroads for transport and supplies. The importance of the rail lines for British transport was not lost on the Boers. At Jacobsdal in early January 1990, the Boer commanders Piet Cronje and Christian De Wet felt secure preparing against a frontal attack only. Although anything in the nature of a turning movement would have rolled up the lines, the commanders were unworried: "The English do not make turning movements. They never leave the railway, because they cannot march."[20] Foreign commentators agreed: "The English have taught him (the Boer) that they are incapable of doing without their railway for a single hour."[21]

The traditional use of artillery in an offensive manner (to "soften" the enemy) also proved ineffective against the Boers. Artillery rarely killed. Invisible pockets of Boer forces would typically be spread over a great distance. Without a target to aim at, long uses of artillery before an attack merely allowed the Boers more time to dig in and study the positioning of the British forces.[22] Furthermore, artillery crews were subject to sniping. At both the first battle of Colenso and the battle of Spion Kop, the British fixation with artillery bombardment resulted in failure.

The most embarrassing failures occurred in the most elite branch—the cavalry. Perhaps the most ingrained of all British military traditions was the charge. For the British soldier, the charge represented a whole way of life.[23] Boers in the open, however, could simply not be pinned, even by a larger British cavalry force: "Constantly harassed, the British would charge only to sustain twenty

---

[19] Fergusson (1984), pp. 114–15.

[20] Sternberg (1901), p. 114.

[21] Stone (1985), p. 140. See also Stone and Schmidl (1988).

[22] As the war began, the British were not only using artillery ineffectively, they were using outdated artillery: some still fired black smoke, alerting the Boers to the position of the British forces. See Stone (1985), p. 312.

[23] Bond (1966), p. 99.

dead troopers and 30–40 dead horses while observing the Boer retreat when still 600 yards distant. The English would then regroup
on their now blown steads as the Boers returned to their irritating
tactic of sniping."[24]

Adaptations in all these arenas were instituted by the British
Army within the first six months of the war. Buller generated
changes in personal equipment immediately. He wrote to Lansdowne before his disastrous defeat at Colenso that in order to re-
store and protect communications at Ladysmith he needed a more
mobile force. To accomplish this, he intended to mount the infantry
and have them wear trousers like the Boers.[25]

After successive defeats, Buller's second attack of Colenso demonstrated significant tactical adaptation.[26] He came to realize that infantry was essential for assault on Boer positions and that half of
the troops should be mounted so as to secure the flanks of the
attacking infantry column and outmaneuver the Boers.[27] Artillery
was used in conjunction with a creeping infantry, and the battle
involved protracted firefights along an extensive front. Roberts's
methods, too, departed significantly from earlier British tactics and
surprised the Boers, who had become confident that the British
would never leave the rails. His first attack at Boer supply lines in
concert with General John French's cavalry on their other side laid
the foundations for a noteworthy success.[28]

Even the cavalry made adjustments. The charge was largely given
up in favor of the firefight. Some brigades even abandoned the
carrying of swords altogether.[29] In addition, military leaders noticed that the cavalry was most effective when combined with the

[24] Stone (1985), p. 358.

[25] Symons (1963), p. 141.

[26] This was fought at the end of February 1900. When Roberts replaced Buller as
commander in chief of the forces in South Africa, he did so without removing Buller
as a field commander.

[27] Stone (1985), p. 166. See also Maurice (1906–10), pp. 509–13.

[28] Packenham (1979), pp. 350–55; Stone (1985), pp. 168–69. Success was delayed
when Roberts fell ill and Kitchener, new to the field, launched a massive frontal
attack on the dug-in Boer forces. After ten days of bombardments against the trapped
Boers, a night attack induced them to surrender. The advantage of the defensive in
this new war, however, was not lost. The British casualties numbered 2,000, the
Boers 87.

[29] Stone (1985), p. 365. Instead of charging the enemy with lances, the British cavalry
began to pursue the Boers with rifle-fire.

mounted infantry. The policy of coupling these two arms was solidified by a War Office study in 1901.[30] Some difficulties, however, were unable to be overcome in the short term. The available rifles either had a short range (carbines) or were large and unwieldy (Lee Enfields). The cavalry was never able to match the Boers, who were both more mobile (with lightweight packs on sturdy ponies) and better shots (with Mausers).

Different factions of the Army drew different lessons from the conventional battles with the Boers. Buller drew the lesson of slower progress with painstaking coordination between artillery, infantry, and mounted troops; Roberts decided to pursue the cheap victories.[31] Roberts's sweep through the capitals demonstrated his understanding of the futility of frontal attacks against the Boers despite Britain's now superior numbers. This sweep, however, by not engaging enemy forces to the degree that Buller had, ultimately left more openings for guerrilla strikes.[32]

Thus, the initial failure of British doctrine was recognized and acted upon by field commanders. Interestingly enough, however, although all field commanders adapted (outside of standard issues of weaponry and clothing), they did not all adapt uniformly. Buller chose to take on the Boers in slow, coordinated movements to defeat the enemy decisively. Roberts chose to capture the capitals and hope for a surrender. Although the initial battles showed the lack of preparation on the part of the British (especially with regard to modern weaponry), the quickness of the field commanders to adapt was noted. G. F. R. Henderson argues, for example, that the extra continental experience of the British and their "general instinct in

[30] Barnett (1970), p. 347; Stone (1985), p. 370. The mounted infantry were more adept at dismounted action. The changes in weaponry (from the lance to the rifle) increased the chances that troops would need to dismount, take cover, and pursue the enemy on the ground.

[31] Stone (1985), p. 174.

[32] There is a fair amount of dispute over the relative success of Buller and Roberts. Some argue that Buller understood the war much better and could have taken it to a better conclusion (see, esp., Packenham 1979). Others hold that Buller was a good second in command but had neither the self-confidence nor the creative capacity to lead an effective campaign. See *Times History of the War in South Africa (1900–1909)* and Symons (1963). Both generals adapted to Boer doctrine albeit in different forms. In order to be successful, however, Roberts's tactics had to be followed by something like Kitchener's policies. Whether Buller would have fared better at preventing the turn toward guerrilla tactics is unknowable.

favor of less rigid methods" caused them to recognize, "even before a short was fired, that what they had practised in peace was utterly unsuited to the Mauser swept battlefield."[33]

Kitchener took the reins from Roberts under a slightly changed cast of civilian characters. In the autumn of 1900, Lord Salisbury reasoned that the war was going well enough to call an election, in which he was victorious. As he put together his new cabinet, however, he decided to give the foreign secretary's job to Lansdowne. (Until this point, Lord Salisbury had been both prime minister and foreign secretary.) Lansdowne's undersecretary, St. John Brodrick, took over the War Office.[34]

Kitchener faced a Boer army with a doctrine not unlike those that have been encountered by world powers since World War II. The Boers' army had always been a highly nationalistic force enjoying the support of the population. The Boers now abandoned all pretense of a conventional war and turned to guerrilla tactics. By exploiting proclamations of amnesty, they turned fighting into a spasmodic business. Apparently peaceful farmers turned into saboteurs and partisans the moment the coast was clear, and the traditional rules of battle were ineffective.

By the time Kitchener took over in the fall of 1900, Milner was exasperated with the military measures pursued since the previous spring. He put the blame for the outburst of guerrilla activity squarely on Roberts:

> The fatal error is not to hold district A and make sure of it before you go on to district B—I mean the fatal error latterly, not at first when you had to rush. The consequence is we have a big army campaigning away in the front and the enemy swarming in the country behind it. . . . But it is no earthly use dashing about any more when there is nothing to get at the end of the dash, and you only wear out your footmen and kill your horses. The time for over-running is over, . . . stage two is a gradual subjugation, district by district, leaving small

[33] Henderson (1905), p. 372.
[34] Ensor (1936).

entrenched and well supplied garrisons behind your columns as they sweep the country and mounted police to patrol between these posts.[35]

Milner held little hope of Kitchener's changing these policies now that Roberts had been called home to replace Wolseley as commander in chief. He thought that Kitchener, too, was in a hurry.

In early March, however, Kitchener came up with a two-pronged strategy to counter the new Boer doctrine: (1) sweeping operations to flush the guerrillas out of large areas of the country and (2) the destruction of anything that could give sustenance to the guerrillas.[36] The strategy was carried out by building a series of blockhouses (fortified huts), within rifle range of one another, to serve as forts from which to defend designated areas. These and barbed wire operated to divide up the countryside into units that could be swept clean. Farms within these areas were burned, and the rural civilian population was placed in internment camps.

Milner was aghast at Kitchener's plan. He thought that the bulk of the population in the new colonies required protection, rather than punishment. He proposed a progressive reconquest of the two colonies by gradually securing each district before tackling the next—slowly occupying the country, bit by bit.[37] Kitchener's policies became equally unpopular with the population at home. The interning of the civilian population, especially, caused an uproar in London. As the war wound down, politicians in Parliament called Kitchener's policies "methods of barbarism." Certainly, this policy cost dearly in human lives and suffering (thousands of people died in the camps of disease due to inadequate facilities and poor sanitation). The ethical questions brought up by the British strategy have been the subject of much debate.

For all its barbarism, however, the policy worked. In contrast to the equally barbarous American search-and-destroy operations, the blockhouses provided a defensive mechanism with which to hold

---

[35] Packenham quotes a letter from Milner to the new secretary of state for war, Sir John Broderick (179), p. 495.

[36] Ibid., p. 522.

[37] Interestingly, the policy Milner proposed was quite similar to the one used by the British in Malaya 45 years later, which provided a blueprint for the counterinsurgency doctrine Kennedy pushed in Vietnam.

on to territory and clear the countryside of guerrillas. Whereas the United States attempted to succeed by killing a percentage of the enemy, the British sought to control territory. Despite Milner's concerns that Kitchener was "in a hurry,"[38] Kitchener instituted a plan that was not quick or easy, or even popular; but it was effective and, ultimately, successful.[39] In April 1902, the Boers entered negotiations to end the war.

What is important for the purpose of testing the institutional model against the conventional wisdom is that the changes instituted by the British were not pushed on a reluctant army by astute civilian leaders in London, but were initiated by the Army itself, often by the commander in the field. Aside from general plans of the campaign, (i.e., which path to take through the Transvaal and the Orange Free State), Buller was given no tactical or doctrinal instructions from Lansdowne.[40] Civilian leaders (the prime minister, the secretary of state for war, and the colonial secretary) in London were uninvolved with changes in doctrine.

The one civilian leader interested in military readiness for South Africa both before and during the conflict was Sir Alfred Milner, high commissioner for South Africa and lieutenant governor of Cape Colony. His concern before the war, although greater than that of the civilians in London, still underestimated the preparations needed by the British and had little effect on the doctrine pursued

[38] There is evidence that Kitchener could have been in a hurry. In March 1901, Broderick cabled to Kitchener that his long-sought-after goal—to be commander in chief in India—would be his once the war was over. See Packenham (1979), p. 521.

[39] This is not to say that Milner's plan would have necessarily been less effective. The similar policy instituted in Malaya worked quite well. Why the British army chose blockhouses and internment camps in 1901 and the protection of the population in New Villages in 1950 is an interesting question that I will return to later.

[40] There is some dispute as to whether Lansdowne did make serious adjustments in the personnel that Buller had to work with. While some scholars indicate that of all the officers that Buller requested, only two were given their proper assignments (Stone and Schmidl 1988, p. 55), others maintain that the War Office consulted with Buller and took his advice in the decisions about his staff (Symons 1963, p. 91). It may be that the personnel Buller wanted were appointed but not always in the right position. Regardless of how we resolve this, it is clear from the removal of Buller that civilian leaders had considerable power over personnel appointments. There is no evidence to suggest, however, that civilians made conscious attempts to generate a particular doctrine through the appointment of personnel.

in the first part of the war. Milner's plan for military doctrine in the second half of the war was passed over for a different, though equally adaptive, doctrine.

The development of civil-military relations discussed in Chapter 2 explains why military leaders created an appropriate doctrine to fight the Boers. In the years before the Boer War, civilian authority had favored military leaders espousing flexible and adaptable responses to immediate threats over those more concerned with the "scientific" doctrine based on the Prussian experience, which was in vogue at the time. Less adaptive military leaders had less impact on British military policy. In this way, civilian control over personnel had affected the bias of the Britain Army. British Army professionalism of this time was much less concerned with standard manners of thinking about war than with adapting these standards to the particulars of British security. This increased the possibility that the British Army would adapt to meet the threats it faced.

## INTERIM REFORMS AND INTERIM PERFORMANCES

However adaptable the British Army was, the Boer War was seen as a testament to British unpreparedness by politicians of the day.[41] Concern was undoubtedly fueled by ever-increasing worries about German power on the continent.[42] A royal commission was set up to investigate military problems in the Boer War and to suggest reforms. As I argued in Chapter 2, these reforms increased the institutional integrity and coherence of the Army and the defense community in general and opened new possibilities for the defense community to advise politicians, but without undermining the ability of unified civilian leadership to direct military performance. In Chapter 2, I also examined the issues involved with British fixation on offensive doctrine in World War I and argued that this was a result of civilian interest in the continent and civilian appointment of offensive-minded ("continentalist") officers.

[41] Much of the criticism directed at the Army after the Boer War revolved around unpreparedness, sloppiness, and a lack of professionalism. Little, if anything, was mentioned about adaptability.
[42] See Chapter 2, n. 57.

The story of the British before World War I demonstrates the synergistic interaction between domestic institutions and the international system discussed in Chapter 1. Perceived failures during the Boer War underscored by new developments in world politics and radical technological advances in naval vessels and rapid-firing guns led British civilian leaders both to take action to coordinate military arms in order to create a better response to anticipated international demands and to appoint those officers interested in continental defense, which had been out of vogue in policy circles. The increasing focus on Germany was coincident with the new structure. Still, these developments took a particular form to maintain cabinet control over military policy. Because of Cabinet control, the military was again unable to use increased international demands to carve out expert spheres of discretion not subject to civilian purview.

In times when the politics of preparedness were less popular, the same control over personnel that brought continental defense to the fore in the pre–World War I days kept the Army from moving as rapidly toward peacetime innovation in the pre–World War II days. This is important for the case of the lack of armored innovation between World War I and World War II. Civilians who are able quickly to intervene in crisis situations may be less likely to try to anticipate (and thus pay for) future contingencies. Although some military leaders in Britain were thinking about how to incorporate armored doctrine, it was not widely accepted or incorporated into war plans until during World War II. As Harold Winton points out, one of the prominent explanations of the failure to develop armor was civilian reluctance to field the costs.[43]

This was not an atypical pattern of British Army adaptation. In neither the Boer War nor the Malayan Emergency did the British Army adapt before the fact. They often, however, managed to alter doctrine in the midst of war. This is a pattern we are more likely to see when civilian control is unified both because unified control increases the chances that the military organization will reward flexibility (and therefore think of new options during a war) and because unified control eases the use of personnel to control the military and thus makes it easier for civilians to intervene in crises

[43] Winton (1988).

situations. In the particular circumstances that faced the British Army (where advanced preparation and spending on warfare readiness was rarely in the electoral interests of politicians), the pattern that developed generally tended to reward flexibility in crisis situations.

## MILITARY DOCTRINE IN MALAYA

It should have been harder for the British military to adapt in Malaya than it was during the Boer War for three reasons. First, the jungle terrain was more difficult to operate in. Second, the post–World War II British Army looked more like a conventional army than it had before the Boer War. It had just finished fighting a conventional war in Europe and remained committed to the defense of Europe as part of the North Atlantic Treaty Organization (NATO). Finally, the political goal in the Malayan Emergency was more clearly tied to nation building than it was in the Boer War, so that the barbarous tactics employed by the Army in South Africa would have clearly been an affront to political goals.

Also, the popular backlash after the Boer War over the methods of barbarism had alerted both civilian and military leaders about changes in the ultimate superior—the voters. The new character of the voting public after the nineteenth-century reform acts took a while to affect Parliament and the Cabinet. Even up to World War I, many would argue, British democracy was still heavily influenced by its aristocratic past.[44] Popular reaction, first to the Boer War and then, in much greater force, to World War I, however, notified leaders about the concerns of the general population that could no longer be ignored. Political leaders would be punished if they saved Malaya by destroying it.[45]

In all these ways, the task facing the British Army in Malaya was similar to that facing the United States in Vietnam.[46] Indeed, the

[44] See Cannadine (1990).

[45] Military leaders in charge of the conflict understood these constraints and created a much gentler counterinsurgency doctrine. The ability of military leaders to learn appropriate lessons from popular reaction to earlier wars and adjust doctrine accordingly attests to the flexibility induced by the British structure of delegation.

[46] A major difference between the United States and the British after World War II was that the British were no longer in the same position of international strength

British Army initially suffered many difficulties similar to problems the United States would later sustain in Vietnam. In the first encounters with the enemy, the British Army suffered problems engaging the enemy due to its concentration of troops—a holdover from the recent European war. As in the Boer War, however, military leaders soon innovated to develop an appropriate doctrine and command-and-control channels that would support the doctrine: "Though many mistakes were made in the early years and the whole process took from 1948 to 1960, the United Kingdom and the Government of Malaya gradually evolved what stands out as an almost classic 'long-haul low-cost' strategy well adapted to the problem they confronted."[47]

Civilian leaders happened to be more interested in discussions of doctrine during the Malayan emergency than they had been during the Boer War. Winston Churchill in 1951 certainly made his preferences about the course of doctrine clearer than Lord Salisbury had in 1900. In so doing, however, it is important to note that he adopted the opinions and advice of his military leaders. Civilian leaders did not intervene in the military organization to force innovation–they endorsed military innovation.[48] Undoubtedly the command-and-control channels that Churchill allowed to be opened for General Sir Gerald Templer were instrumental in facilitating a more successful counterinsurgency doctrine. The innovations, however (even the suggestions for changes in the command-and-control instruments), came from the military leaders themselves.

## The Background

The Malayan Communist party (MCP) grew out of an anticolonial movement. Throughout the 1930s the party was active among Chinese students and labor organizations, promoting anticolonialist

---

and leadership. A balance-of-power analyst might argue that after World War II, the extension of the United States' nuclear umbrella to NATO countries freed the British to concentrate on lesser threats. It is for this reason that I set up the comparison between the Boer War and Vietnam. Still, if it can be demonstrated that the same dynamics were at work in the Malayan case, the institutional argument is strengthened.

[47] Komer (1972), p. v.

[48] Rosen (1991) argues that this is the most effective form of civilian intervention.

demonstrations and labor strikes. Its base of support in the Chinese community grew increasingly concerned with Japanese penetration of China after 1937 and modified its anticolonial rhetoric to focus on the Japanese threat. The British even supported the MCP and provided it with weapons to fight the Japanese as the threat increased. When the Japanese invasion of Southeast Asia drove the British colonials out, the MCP organized a guerrilla army to fight the Japanese. After the Japanese capitulated, the communists resisted the reestablishment of British rule and British-supported government of Malaya control. When negotiations failed to bring a satisfactory solution, the MCP turned to insurgency. On June 19, 1948 a "State of Emergency" was declared by the British high commissioner, and military action began.[49]

## The Military Response

A number of emergency regulations were put into effect immediately. The first was a requirement that the entire population over twelve years of age register at police stations and have photographs and thumbprints recorded on identity cards. These cards were necessary to obtain food, certain grants, rights to live in a resettled village, and other advantages. The regulations also provided the government with the power to arrest and detain without a trial, the power to impose curfews, and the right to search private property without a permit.[50]

Initial British forces included a brigade of Gurkhas (six battalions

[49] The particularities of the Malayan population influenced the course of the war. Roughly one-half of the population are indigenous Malay, and the indigenous government was composed of Malay sultans. When Malaya was colonized, the British imported Chinese laborers, who grew to be one-third of the population. The remainder of the population is of Indian descent (also imported to work by the British). The support for the communists came almost exclusively from the Chinese population. This, some have argued, made the counterinsurgency easier. Not all the Chinese supported the insurgency, however. In fact, by the time the emergency began, the majority of nonforeign economic activity was being conducted by a percentage of the Chinese population. So the British could not simply round up the Chinese, for fear of disrupting the fledgling economy. Also, the beginnings of what would become serious ethnic tensions between the ruling Malays and the economically powerful Chinese had already shown themselves. The British had to tread lightly to avoid inciting these tensions.

[50] See Dewar (1984), pp. 31–33; Komer (1972), pp. 34–38.

stationed in Malaya and one in Singapore), three British infantry battalions and a gunner regiment.[51] These forces were never placed in control of the insurgency effort. They were called upon to support the police and civil authorities. A senior police officer, W. N. Grey, was placed in charge of expanding both the police and military forces. Grey ended up spending all of his time coordinating the police, however, and military commanders took the lead in operations. Informal committees at the state level (usually consisting of the chief police officer, the British advisor to the local sultan, the sultan's prime minister, and the local army commander) were inadept at providing proper coordination for operations, especially in the area of intelligence gathering.

Although the emergency provisions resulted in an initial drop in guerrilla activity, by 1950 rising terrorist incidents convinced the British government that changes were required.[52] Lieutenant General Sir Harold Briggs (recently retired) was placed in a new position called director of operations directly under the high commissioner. His job was to plan, coordinate, and direct the operations of the police and military forces (now increased to include nine British units, six Gurkha, and two Malay).[53]

The major innovation begun by Briggs was a system of New Villages. Even with the emergency provisions, the guerrillas were still managing to supply themselves through contact with squatters on the fringe of the jungle. Briggs's plan was to resettle some 425,000 squatters (most of them Chinese) into New Villages. He proposed that by both moving these people out of guerrilla reach and improving their standard of living, he could make supporting the government a more attractive proposition and increase the flow of information to the government forces.

Briggs set up a system of war executive committees, which connected the central government to the states and districts for the coordination of the counterinsurgency effort. At the top of the pyramid was the Federal War Council, which included Briggs, the high

---

[51] Dewar (1984), p. 30.

[52] This stands in sharp contrast to the evaluation of success of American efforts in Vietnam. The rise of terrorist incidents in late 1959 (including the week of Tet—January 18–25, 1960—when 26 local officials were killed in Long An Province) were all but ignored by the American military organization. See Race (1972), pp. 113–40.

[53] Dewar (1984), p. 33.

commissioner, the chief secretary, the federation secretary of defense, the police commissioner, the general officer commanding Malaya, and the air officer commanding Malaya.[54]

Each of the nine Malay states had a counterpart State War Executive Committee (SWEC). The state committees were chaired by the prime minister to the local sultan and included representatives from the police, military, and British civil service as well as community representatives where appropriate. At the state level, there was also an operations subcommittee, which met more frequently to assess and implement actions. Finally, there was a similar committee at the district level, the District War Executive Committee (DWEC). Again, police, military and civilian government representatives as well as information officers were included.[55]

This committee system provided important governmental infrastructure. The SWECs and DWECs were useful for implementing the New Village policy. The state and district committees ordered police and military operations, controlled food supplies, set curfews, and handled resettlement decisions, information and psychological warfare operations, and the like. By facilitating coordination, they allowed a quick and educated response to local problems. They also kept key officials informed at each operating level and both forced civilian officials to be involved with emergency implementation and allowed them to review military operations.[56] The committee system bypassed inflexible staff systems (particularly at the state level) and gave more of a role to commanders and executives.[57] The infrastructure provided by the committee system allowed the New Village policy to be implemented effectively.

This is not to suggest that the New Village policy was a popular one. The rural Chinese citizens regarded the policy with ambivalence. Although some were anxious to escape the problems of being harassed by the police, the army, and the guerrillas and thought that resettlement offered opportunities for upward advancement, many felt that the disadvantages of moving far outweighed the advantages. The New Villages were chosen with security considera-

---

[54] Komer (1972), pp. 27–28.
[55] Ibid., p. 28.
[56] Ibid., p. 29.
[57] Stubbs (1989), p. 99.

tions in mind, not farming. Resettlers had to spend time and effort building new homes and working less productive land with minimal compensation.[58]

There are two important contrasts between the New Villages and the Strategic Hamlet policy initiated by the United States in South Vietnam. First, the New Villages did offer some benefits to the resettlers: in the Vietnamese case, the resettlers were actually forced to buy the materials for their new homes. Second, the committee system allowed the policy to be effective, at least on the security dimension: whereas the resettled Vietnamese were forced to endure many hardships often without any increase in security, the New Villagers were not subject to the same security problems after their moves.

Even with the committee system in effect, however, Briggs encountered difficulties prompting army and police units to follow his directions. Also, the committees provided a lot of checks on action (i.e., civilian on military, police on each) that Briggs felt hindered his command authority. He declared that he had not been wholly satisfied with his powers and urged the British government to give greater power to his successor. The increase in terrorist activity (probably a result of guerrilla anger with the New Villages) and the assassination of Sir Henry Gurney (high commissioner, the senior civilian position in the colonies) prompted the new Conservative government in Britain to respond to Briggs's request.[59]

Upon Gurney's death the secretary of state for the colonies, Oliver Lyttleton, took a trip to Malaya to assess first-hand the state of the conflict.[60] He met with a number of people, including Briggs, who urged him to appoint a military leader of proven capacity and national fame to direct all aspects of the campaign. By the end of his tour, Lyttleton had come to the conclusion that Briggs's recommendations should be followed. General Sir Gerald Templer, former vice chief of the imperial staff, was chosen to hold the merged posts of high commissioner and director of operations.[61]

Templer embarked on his mission in Malaya with both Cabinet

---

[58] Ibid., pp. 102–7.

[59] Gurney was assassinated on October 6, 1951.

[60] Lyttleton was new to the job. Winston Churchill, who became prime minister in the same month that Gurney was assassinated, named him to the post.

[61] Dewar (1984), p. 35; Komer (1972), p. 30; Stubbs (1989), pp. 134–48.

approval and a directive emanating from the prime minister.[62] The directive, although strongly worded, changed little of the British mission, but it gave Templer the power to "assume complete operational command over all the Armed Forces assigned to operations in the Federation" and "to issue operational orders to their commanders without reference to the Commander in Chief, Far East."[63]

More important than the wording of the directive was the power over personnel that it offered to Templer. He began with a large percentage of new personnel at the upper levels of administration.[64] He appointed two chief assistants—General Sir Robert Lockhart as deputy director of operations and D.C. McGillivray as deputy high commissioner.[65] Furthermore, Templer used his unique powers to galvanize the counterinsurgency effort, transferring officers who did not measure up.[66] He also made minor administrative changes by merging the Federal War Council with the Federal Executive Council to underscore the fusion of civil and military efforts against the communists.

These actions were underpinned by Templer's perspective on how to conduct a counterguerrilla campaign. First, he reemphasized Briggs's point that it was wrong to separate emergency activities from day to day government. Second, he considered the guerrilla war to be a battle for the hearts and minds of the population. The answer to defeating the guerrillas, Templer believed, lay in cultural, political, economic, and spiritual (in addition to military) factors. He was given wide power by the government in London to follow this inclination. Finally, Templer spent a great deal of energy gathering information. He traveled constantly with a small staff of advisors and a military escort. He met with everyday villagers in many parts

[62] While the high commissioner needed to be approved by the Colonial Office, the merging of the offices of high commissioner and director of operations had to be approved by the Cabinet as a whole.

[63] Stubbs (1989), p. 141. For the text of the directive, see Purcell (1954), pp. 86–87.

[64] The director of intelligence, Sir William Jenkin, had submitted his resignation shortly after Gurney's death. More important, the commissioner of police, W. N. Grey, with whom Briggs had repeated problems, also submitted his resignation. See Stubbs (1989), p. 138.

[65] Komer (1972), p. 30. Lockhart had briefly been director of operations after Briggs left and before Templer took over. MacGillivray's appointment was not without controversy, especially among the Malays who thought that a Malay should have been appointed to fill this post. See Stubbs (1989), p. 142.

[66] Komer (1972), p. 31.

of the country over the course of his tenure and often used unorthodox tactics for information gathering.

On pure military matters, Templer reinforced Briggs's principle that large-scale operations be forsworn in favor of small ones. Army personnel were never deployed as divisions and only infrequently as brigades or even battalions. They operated from "company bases" in platoon-or even smaller-size units.[67] The Army (particularly the infantry) made the main contribution to the war in Malaya. Air power was used primarily for supply. Offensive air strikes were thought to be, at best, unproductive, at worst, detrimental to the British cause.[68]

There was certainly resistance, at least initially, from individual Army commanders: "The Army had never felt comfortable in their role of supporting the civil power; they were soldiers, many of them said, fighting with one arm tied behind their backs."[69] Particularly, the coordination of the police and the army presented difficulties. However, the overwhelming operational control given to the director of operations under Briggs and then subsidized by control over personnel under Templer made it possible to circumvent these difficulties. Although the military retained their control over their troops and were responsible for their administration, training, and support, operational control was in the hands of the executive committees. The intermediate division commands almost never played a tactical role.[70]

The ability of British Army leaders to think about counterinsurgency as a civil-military effort was crucial to the success of counterinsurgency in Malaya. Similar policies in the form of Strategic Hamlets were regarded as outside the bounds of "military" by the U.S. Army in Vietnam. The U.S. Army's lack of attention to either the importance of internal security in the hamlets or the detrimental effects of bombing on the population in the hamlets contributed significantly to failure in the implementation of the policy. By 1953, food denial became the chief basis of military operations. The stringent clamp-down on food supplies to the guerrillas in a given area

[67] Ibid., p. 50.
[68] Ibid., p. 51.
[69] H. Miller (1954), p. 137.
[70] Komer (1972), p. 48.

over many months allowed troops and police to drive the guerrillas to risk coming out of hiding and exposing themselves to ambush and patrols.[71]

## *The Malayan Emergency and the Vietnam War Compared*

Although the historical differences between the Malayan Emergency and the Vietnam War, of course matter, they are not so great as to make the cases noncomparable—especially with regard to the adaptation of the military. One might argue that the ethnic variable made the British job in Malaya easier than the American job in Vietnam. After all, the British did not have to pay attention to the Malay population; they could simply focus on the Chinese. Thus it was easier to identify the enemy. This line of argument, however, ignores an important complication of ethnic politics in Malaya. The Chinese population was not only the source of the communist insurgency, it was also the economic backbone of the country. Indiscriminate use of force against the Chinese population could undermine economic growth. The fact that a portion of the Chinese population in Malaya was economically powerful while another portion was behind the communist insurgency and the fact that the entire Chinese population was politically weak complicated, rather than eased, the task of the British in Malaya.[72]

In a different vein, one could argue that the British colonial experience in Malaya increased British ability to integrate military measures with measures to support the population. Undoubtedly, this is true. However, three considerations lead me to discount this factor as a complete explanation for successful military adaptation by the British in Malaya: First, the French experience in Vietnam certainly did not seem to support their ability to integrate these two measures. Second, the British did have to work at creating an adequate doctrine, as their initial efforts were not successful. Finally, having to work with the sovereign government in Vietnam did not prevent the U.S. Marines from successfully adapting in the I Corp area of South Vietnam (as I argued in Chapter 4).

[71] Ibid., p. 51.

[72] For general comments on the dilemmas of the ethnic and economic mix in Malaya (and then Malaysia), see Means (1976), Milne and Mauzy (1977), Stenson (1980), and Vorys (1976).

Certainly, the South Vietnamese government was (and would have been, regardless of the Army's level of adaptation) an issue in the overall success of the U.S. mission to defend South Vietnam from communist incursion. And even if the U.S. Army *had* adapted, the ultimate success of U.S. policy would have been affected (most probably hindered) by the behavior of the South Vietnamese government. Nonetheless, I think it is hard to argue that this was a significant issue in preventing the Army from adapting to the communist threat in Vietnam.

Another potential explanation for the British success examines the role of qualified individuals. William Slim, for example, who was field marshall during the Malayan Emergency, had fought effectively against the Japanese to retake Burma during World War II. His experience in non-European war was important, as is demonstrated by his first action as chief of the Imperial General Staff, when he threatened to resign if action were taken to reduce the terms of service in the British Army from 18 months to 12 months, which Slim thought would be particularly disruptive to those men who served in Hong Kong or Malaya.

I do not think that Slim's experience and position alone, however, can explain British adaptation. After all, the British did struggle in the opening rounds of the Malayan conflict. Jungle conflict against the Japanese was different from jungle warfare against an insurgent communist force. Especially at the mid-level of command, there was an initial tendency to try to meet the enemy in regular battle engagements that led the British Army to miss the insurgents.[73] As the war progressed, there continued to be mid-level resistance to the close cooperation between military, civilian, and police groups necessary to protect increasing amounts of the population. This resistance was not overcome until the end of 1951, when Templer was given extreme powers over personnel and a personal directive from the prime minister and the cabinet.

Still, the appointment of Slim is important as evidence of the structure of the British Army and how professionalism in the British Army differed from professionalism in the American Army. Service in the jungles of Burma was not a dead end for an officer aspiring to the highest echelons of the British Army. One must note that the

[73] See, esp., Komer (1972) but also O'Ballance (1966).

American officer who had served with Slim in Burma, Richard G. Stilwell, although employed as an advisor and highly critical evaluator of the Army's efforts during the initial years in Vietnam, did not have near the career opportunities that were available to Slim. Because the path to prominence in the American Army was through Europe, not through Burma, there was a perverse logic to crisis situations in peripheral areas, as James Thompson points out.[74] As crises developed in Vietnam, higher-level officers were brought into the decision-making process; but because these higher-level officers garnered most of their experience in European contingencies, there was an *increased* chance that the situation would be misunderstood, the higher up the ladder you went.

So while Slim's position alone was not a determining factor in making adaptation to counterinsurgency easier, it does demonstrate a structure of professionalism that biased toward, rather than against, understanding different contingencies. Both the structure of professionalism (a product of past civilian actions) and the structure of civilian authority and oversight led to the successful adaptation of the British Army in Malaya.

In Malaya, as in the Boer War, military leaders did not resist innovation to counterinsurgency doctrine. Even operating in a difficult terrain at a time when the British Army was used to fighting large enemies in Europe (and Asia), the British Army leaders were able to overcome resistance to adaptation by lower-level personnel with a delegated restructuring of authority.

As in the Boer War, the impetus for innovation in Malaya came from the military leaders in charge of the conflict. Although civilians (namely, Churchill and Lyttleton) took more interest in military doctrine than had Lord Salisbury at the turn of the century, they cannot be credited with doctrinal innovations. The innovations came at the hands of the military leaders in command of the emergency. Civilian leaders continued to use control over personnel, however, to reinforce incentives for military leaders to innovate. Control over personnel for oversight was used initially by the Cabinet and then passed to a civil-military agent in Malaya—the high commissioner/director of operations. General Templer continued to use this mechanism to

[74] J. Thompson (1989).

[127]

transfer personnel who did not measure up to the standards he set for counterinsurgency.

The unification of civilian authority and the use of personnel appointments for oversight that it afforded the prime minister was similar in the Boer War and in Malaya. There were changes in both the ultimate principal (the voters) and the military organizations from the time of the Boer War to the Malayan Emergency. The public reaction to the Army's tactics in the Boer War alerted politicians to the political costs of allowing the military to use brutal means to achieve their goals. In Malaya, then, we see greater sensitivity to working with the local population.[75] Also, the reforms initiated after the Boer War created greater coherence in the Army. Thus, we do not see vast differences between the ways different military leaders prosecuted the war in Malaya. The reforms also gave the prime minister more avenues for information, which encouraged a greater interest in military doctrine.[76]

In the Malayan case, we see the doctrinal outcome of the way the structure of civilian leadership affected the configuration of professionalism in Britain. By the time of the Malayan Emergency, British military professionals had developed a wider range of options in thinking about how to approach war than had U.S. military professionals. This led them, with little difficulty, to think of ways to adapt a very conventional army to fight a very unconventional war. The unification of civilian leadership eased the military leaders' task by opening easy avenues for constructing significant changes in command-and-control channels, which allowed the leaders to induce lower-level military personnel to change their tactics.

British military leaders adapted to both of the threats we have examined in this chapter so as to create a doctrine that was integrated with the country's national security policy. In the Boer War, especially, the Army adapted despite a general neglect of military doctrine by the civilian leaders. In the Malayan Emergency, there is

---

[75] Working with the population was also facilitated by the history of British colonial administration in Malaya. See Clutterbuck (1966), O'Ballance (1966), and Pye (1956).

[76] Undoubtedly, some of the difference between the level of involvement in military doctrine between Lord Salisbury and Churchill is purely a function of personality or personal interest. Churchill was simply more interested in doctrine than was Lord Salisbury.

more interest on the part of civilian leaders, but the locus of innovation comes from the military leaders.

The development of civil-military relations in Britain traced in Chapter 2 explains how institutionally unified civilian leaders affected the course of professionalization in Britain to create incentives for military leaders to be sensitive to the intricacies of particular conflicts. Continued civilian control over personnel has been an easy mechanism to maintain a bias toward flexibility in the British Army. Those officers who adapt to the security contingencies British politicians define as important are more likely to succeed professionally.

These two cases demonstrate two points about the oversight structure in Britain and its effect on military response to political goals. First, the British experience in the Boer War demonstrates that unified civilian leadership is likely to make it unnecessary for civilians to intervene to force the military to innovate. Military leaders are more likely to anticipate civilian goals. Second, if civilians do intervene, they are more likely to get what they want, because it is easier for civilian leaders to appoint military leaders who agree with them than to change the behavior of those who do not.[77] The risk in this type of system is with civilian mistakes or civilian preoccupation with political, rather than international, goals. We have seen examples of this type of problem both in the source of the offensive doctrine in World War I and in the lack of armored innovations before World War II.

---

[77] If Posen ever appears to be right, it will be in a case of unified authority like the British case, because this is the structure of delegation most likely to lead to effective civilian intervention. Indeed, the two cases he uses successfully in his book—the British and the Germans (under Hitler)—are cases of unified authority. Furthermore, John Mearsheimer's account of the development of the Blitzkrieg supports the contention that is it through control of personnel that civilian leaders can most easily affect the course of military doctrine (1983, chap. 4).

# [6]

## Conclusion

This book examined why two countries that occupied similar places in the international system and comparable grand strategies had such different success as they responded to similar threats. Domestic institutions hold the key to explaining the variation in military doctrine. The structure of domestic institutions both affects the bias of military organizations and indicates the type of civilian intervention which will be most likely to prompt military change. Both these factors are significant in determining how readily military organizations will adapt doctrine to meet new circumstances.

Military organizations will be responsive to civilian goals when military leaders expect to be rewarded for that responsiveness. Military leaders' expectations depend on how civilian leaders have chosen to set up and monitor military organizations. A country's institutional structure influences the electoral imperatives of civilian leaders and thus their choices about how to delegate responsibility to military organizations. Individuals' short-term strategies for retaining their institutional position and power filter their substantive policy aims and influence both civilian and military leaders' interpretations of the international system—and thus their perspectives on national security.

In particular, in the cases examined here, civilian leaders in Britain, who had institutional incentives to act as a unit, had an easier time agreeing on both policy goals and oversight options to ensure that the Army followed these goals. Under these conditions, the British Army reacted more flexibly to changes in civilian leaders' goals.[1] Conversely, civilian leaders in the United States, who had institutional incentives to act separately, found it harder to agree on policy goals and often chose more complex oversight mechanisms, which did not always induce the U.S. Army to respond easily to change.

Policy outcomes, however, could not be deduced from the unity or division of the institutional structures alone. The oversight mechanisms that civilians chose were also biased by historical lessons often contained in the electoral politics of the time.[2] Similarly, knowing the oversight mechanism did not give us an absolute purchase on the policy outcome. Policy was a product of the way the oversight mechanism worked within a particular political context.

Divided civilian institutions in the United States led to more reliance on budgets to control military organizations.[3] Budgetary control led military organizations in the United States to develop high levels of integrity after the Civil War and to have more discretion in the formative stages of professionalization over the standards of merit in each military organization. The Army, particularly, used this discretion to indulge its fascination with (and belief in the usefulness of) Prussian-originated "military science." Doctrine in the Army reflected this concern with abstract principles, rather than the particular circumstances of a conflict.

In the postwar United States, congressional reliance on the interservice rivalry over budgetary allocations as a mechanism for inducing strategic innovations combined with the particularities of the containment doctrine to reinforce the Army's doctrinal bias toward preparation for a conventional-style war in Europe. This oversight

---

[1] Of course, these goals may not always be those dictated by the international system. The first tier of delegation (between voters and civilian leaders) influences how civilian leaders will interpret the international system. If the dictates of the international system conflict with the short-term political interests of civilian leaders, those leaders will be less likely to promote the requisite changes.

[2] *Electoral politics* is a concise term for "doing what is necessary to stay in power in a democracy." Although, the short-term power requirements might be more difficult to operationalize, this model could also be useful for examining nondemocratic settings.

[3] There were instances in the nineteenth century when other mechanisms, such as presidential control over personnel and congressional support of the militia, were used to exert civilian control over the Army. These mechanisms were used less as the potential political cost of using them increased (in the case of personnel) or the political appeal of using them declined (in the case of the militia).

mechanism induced the Army to innovate in response to changes in technology important to the European context but reinforced its resistance to changes important for other contexts.[4]

Presidents in the United States were discouraged from using radical personnel measures (such as firing military leaders in the midst of war or reaching down into the ranks for appointments) to direct changes in military doctrine, because of the political risks this mechanism presented. Instead, their attempts to induce change were attempts at micromanagement. As we would expect, micromanagement efforts were subject to agency loss. Although the relative success at micromanagement depended on the relative expertise of the president in military matters, micromanagement generally either was ineffective or produced unexpected outcomes.[5]

The Army did not adapt to the situation in Vietnam (despite significant presidential efforts) because its historical development had created a professional bias, embedded in promotion policies, that caused Army leaders to focus on a narrow definition of "military" that excluded much of what was important to counterinsurgency doctrine. Congressional budgetary controls only reinforced the Army's concern with offensive-style European warfare. Presidential

[4] For an example of successful presidential intervention in front-line doctrine, see Art and Ockenden (1981). They argue that (1) presidential intervention was necessary for the development of the cruise missile, (2) the development of the cruise missile occurred in spite of (not because of) the pulling and hauling of bureaucratic agencies, and (3) Congress's role in the micromanagement of defense policy did not change as much as many have assumed it did after the heightening of congressional responsibility for defense in the wake of Vietnam. Interestingly for my model, in their analysis the executive was most successful when he had Congress as an ally in his fights with the service branches to fund the cruise missile program, which the services were not eager to pursue. When Congress questioned the usefulness of the land-attack version of the tactical antiship missile, Defense Department officials had a harder time forcing the Navy's hand.

[5] It is interesting to compare Eisenhower, Kennedy, and Johnson on this count. Eisenhower knew enough not to try to micromanage the military. Kennedy—less of an expert but knowledgeable on military matters—knew what he wanted the military to do but was unsuccessful in making it change. Johnson, neither an expert nor knowledgeable, had to rely on military information in his attempts to induce change and had the worst of all outcomes: he unintentionally encouraged such things as the Army's use of body counts and the separation of the political and military wars while ostensibly trying to get the Army to adapt to insurgent warfare. For an argument that makes predictions about foreign policy outcomes dependent on the relative expertise of the president, see Gronich (1989). For my comment on her model, see Chapter 2, n. 42.

micromanagement failed. The Army's control over setting the indicators for success even made it more difficult for civilians to recognize other service branches' adaptations as successful.

Even if civilian leaders had recognized the success of other branches, the division of control between civilian branches made presidents wary of replacing personnel to change doctrine. Because it was unlikely that any branch but the Army would control doctrine or that the Army would adopt counterinsurgency doctrine, we should have expected the U.S. response to the communist threat in Vietnam to be inappropriate.

The development of civil-military institutions in Britain led British civilian leaders to rely on personnel measures for oversight much more freely than their U.S. counterparts. Control over personnel generated more concern with civilian goals on the part of military leaders, on both an individual and an institutional basis. Individually, officers who were worried about their careers had more incentives to pay attention to civilian goals because civilian leaders held direct power over their jobs. Institutionally, selection of more adaptable leaders for high posts during the Army's professionalization led British military professionalism to incorporate a standard of flexibility. Thus, civilian leaders in Britain had both easier mechanisms to induce military adaptations (they could fire recalcitrant officers without fear of political retribution) and a built-in institutional mechanism for inducing adaptability (British military professionalism reflected a concern with political goals). Civilian leaders' expertise in military matters was less important for successful adaptation, because micromanagement was unnecessary in Britain.

## DELEGATION AND CIVIL-MILITARY RELATIONS

The prevailing national security literature examines civil-military relations as the key to military doctrine. While I agree with this focus, my analysis has demonstrated that the predominant literature on civil-military relations is not adequate to explain the British and American cases. Contrary to the received wisdom on civil-military relations, this book establishes that civilian intervention is neither a necessary, nor a sufficient, condition for military adaptation.

Not all military organizations respond in the same way to similar problems. Neither the British Army at the turn of the century nor the U.S. Marines resisted change the way the U.S. Army did. An adequate model of civil-military relations must allow us to account for variation between the standard responses of different military organizations. The new economics-of-organizations literature has suggested that we examine the terms by which power is delegated to organizations to understand this variation. In other words, its analysts pay attention to the original deal (or setup of the organization) and how this deal is monitored and enforced. These terms affect individual expectations, which hold the key to whether organizations become attached to standard operating procedures, what those standard operating procedures are, and the degree to which career patterns reflect organizational, rather than political, motivations. The terms of delegation help us develop expectations about when organizations will be incremental and slow to change and when they will deal with change more effectively.[6]

The contrast between the ease with which British Army leaders adapted to the Boer threat in South Africa and the communist threat in Malaya and the difficulty the U.S. Army had understanding the war in Vietnam has provided an illustration of this dynamic. Because British politicians promoted leaders who responded to the immediate threats in the empire without large and expensive preparations, military education placed a premium on adapting meager means to meet whatever might threaten the empire. Furthermore, the Cabinet's control over personnel gave incentives to Army leaders interested in their careers to pay attention to political leaders' goals. The terms of delegation to the British Army included civilian control measures that induced the army to pay attention to what civilian leaders wanted.

Because the terms of delegation to the U.S. Army required coordination between two branches of government, the civilian control measures these two branches could agree upon did not induce the Army to pay attention to what any one leader wanted. At different points in American history, the Army has paid more or less attention

---

[6] Bendor (1988); Bendor, Taylor, and Gaalen (1987); March and Olsen (1984); Miller and Moe (1985); Moe (1990).

to Congress or the president.[7] But in the post–World War II era, congressional budgetary control has been the most important factor, partly because it has reinforced the Army's long-standing bias. A lack of civilian agreement upon (and interest in) directing the Army as it became professionalized allowed the U.S. army to develop a strong bias toward abstract principles of war, which left the Army less likely to consider the specific characteristics of any particular conflict.

Not only is civilian intervention neither necessary nor sufficient to promote change, it is not always directed toward objective international demands. As the American politics literature has demonstrated, leaders cannot be depended upon to act in the national interest if the action threatens their domestic power base.[8] A policy product (or a particular action) depends on the domestic benefits it provides to political actors as well as the international benefits it accords to the country.[9]

This dynamic affects both civilian advice and how military organizations respond to civilian intervention. Civilian advice can be politically rather than (or in addition to being) internationally driven. Equally important, military leaders will expect civilian leaders not to commit political suicide but to act within their electoral constraints. Control mechanisms that require political leaders to operate outside their electoral considerations will be less effective both because civilians will be less likely to use them and because military leaders will not expect them to be used. International variables are important in this account, not because they play a determinative role but because they provide political actors with strategic resources.

## INSTITUTIONAL THEORY AND ITS IMPLICATIONS

An earlier wave of theorists concerned with civil-military relations also paid attention to the variations in political institutions. These

---

[7] Thus, American politics experts have asserted forcefully that one must pay attention to Congress as well as the president in order to explain foreign policy outcomes (see, e.g., O'Halloran 1990).

[8] See, e.g., Fiorina (1989), Jacobson (1983), Mayhew (1974), and the selection of essays in Mathew McCubbins and Terry Sullivan (1987).

[9] Snyder's (1984) and Van Evera's (1985) analyses of the roots of the offensive bias before World War I both pay careful attention to these forces.

analysts saw institutional constraints as influences on action, but the focus of this literature was on how individual statesmen manipulated the process of government.[10] It was argued that in the U.S. system of government in which power is dispersed, consensus is derived through persuasion. Policy reflects the process of building consensus as much as it does the merits of one proposal versus another: "The test of policy is not that it will most effectively accomplish an agreed-upon value but that a wider number of people decide to endorse it."[11]

My analysis builds on the earlier wave of political theorizing. By relying on the formal logic of microeconomic theories of delegation, however, it has systematically examined the effect of institutional arrangements on both the development of military organizations and military policy outcomes. This approach avoids some of the pitfalls of the earlier literature, which overemphasized policy formation as opposed to implementation. This stress allowed analysts to understand how much leaders anticipated the reaction of voters but not always how much leaders also anticipated the reaction of organizations. Some analysts in this camp noted the institutional effects of the separation of powers but tended to mix these effects together with ideological factors, leaving unclear the implications for reform.[12]

In particular, many earlier analysts of Vietnam have tended to blame civilian leaders for failed foreign policy because they seemed to be worried more about getting reelected rather than about making good policy.[13] Because political leaders must get reelected in order to pursue their policy goals, we should not expect civilian leaders to sacrifice their electoral chances in order to make good foreign policy. When electoral and international incentives clash, we should expect politicians to choose goals that cater to the demands of the international system but design policies to pursue the goals in such a way as to minimize any political impact—even if such a

[10] Robert Art (1985) has labeled the following analysts the first wave of bureaucratic or "political" perspectives on foreign policy making: Huntington (1957), Hilsman (1967), Neustadt (1980), Schilling, Hammond, and Snyder (1962). One could also add Gelb and Betts (1979) and a number of the early works on the Vietnam War.

[11] Hilsman (1967), p. 365, quoted in Art (1985), p. 469.

[12] See esp., Huntington (1957, 1968).

[13] Berman (1982), Elsberg (1971).

design significantly reduces the policy's effectiveness. The institutional approach tells us the range of policy outcomes we can expect *given* the constraints of electoral politics.

Furthermore, it is not always clear that the policy failure is determined by its formation. Civilian leaders were criticized for gradualism in their Vietnam policy, but the failure of the Army to adapt induced leaders to choose a gradual approach. The *implementation* of policy by the Army in Vietnam was also responsible for the failure of foreign policy. Although the actions of civilian leaders certainly influenced the direction that the implementation of policy in Vietnam took, their control over military doctrine in Vietnam per se was neither direct nor, arguably, intentional. For example, although Congress set up between the service branches the competition that induced the Army to focus on Europe, individual members of Congress did not actively thwart Army innovation in counterinsurgency, nor did they necessarily realize that the structure they had designed restricted the range of Army innovation in Vietnam.

A focus on the terms of delegation, which are conditioned by electoral as well as substantive concerns, alerts us to the possibility of agency loss. It also suggests conditions under which agency losses arise. For instance, it reminds us that policymakers will often choose agency losses in order to avoid electoral costs. Either Kennedy or Johnson might have been able to induce the Army to change had either been willing dramatically to alter the Army leadership, but the electoral costs of such a move prevented its consideration.[14] This was not, however, a result of weakness of resolve on the part of Kennedy or Johnson. The system was designed to prevent the consideration of such political maneuvers. The United States' structure of accountability ensures that politicians will conduct military oversight in a more cumbersome manner.

This analysis also rests on assumptions about how the trade-off between short- and long-term goals affects an actor's perceptions. Many students of psychological theory have examined the tendencies that underlie this assumption. Robert Jervis, for example, argues that cognitive consistency rules, which generally provide rational ways to make decisions while minimizing the amount of information

---

[14] Although, as Rosen (1991) has pointed out, military mavericks often fail to command the support necessary to institute real change.

an individual must process, can prompt "irrational consistency," when an actor is faced with a conflict between a desired outcome and its cost, or two desired outcomes. The chances of irrational consistency are highest, Jervis argues, when the trade-offs are easy to avoid or especially painful.[15]

Policy consequences are always hard to predict, and electoral losses are almost always painful.[16] An individual who suspects that a particular policy will be detrimental to his or her political interests will be less likely to believe that the policy is necessary for national security. Leaders will be most likely to make good national security policy when they do not need to make a trade-off between their electoral fortunes and the international fortunes of their country. The institutional structure, by influencing the range of short-term interests, can allow us to project the boundaries of long-term ambitions. The institutional design can either enhance or ease this trade-off.[17]

The focus on delegation eases our ability systematically to analyze foreign policy in a comparative fashion. By directing our attention toward politicians designing or manipulating institutions to maintain or enhance their electoral advantage, it alerts us to how differences in political structures promote different policy outcomes. This helps us to understand both the growth and change of domestic institutions over time, and the impact of institutions on particular policy questions.[18]

Because institutions develop over time and what happens at time 1 affects the possible outcomes at time 2, this model makes no absolute predictions free from historical context. We should not expect that divided government will always produce the same outcomes in different settings. For example, the electoral system that influences party discipline is very important for determining the effects of di-

---

[15] Trade-offs are easy to avoid when the values involved are vague and ill defined, money (which facilitates comparisons) is not involved, or the effects of the action are hard to predict. See Jervis (1976), p. 144; see also Akerlof (1984).

[16] I use electoral losses only, for simplicity. Other professional losses (risking being passed up for promotion, etc.) follow the same logic.

[17] Although institutions are designed in order to encourage behavior that is consistent with long-term goals, institutional architects cannot always anticipate future problems.

[18] Pierson (1993).

vided government. If party discipline is very strong, the effects of divided civilian institutions will be mediated.

Also, the effects of the institutional structure on an organization depends on the position of the organization. Some organizations, such as the CIA, are created to ease the effects of divided institutions. The CIA was not subject to the same kinds of congressional fiscal review as military organizations were. At other times, actions taken by civilian leaders for one purpose (e.g., the constant review of whether the United States needed a separate Marine force) can accidentally induce an adaptive organization. In the case of the Marines, constant review prompted the organization to develop promotion policies that encouraged its leaders to be responsive to civilian goals.

The institutional logic, however—once set within a particular context—can give us substantial purchase on policy outcomes. Differences in institutional structures that affect ensuing differences in the growth of parties, the issue-focus of voters, the interpretation of the international system, and the terms of delegation will lead to differences in the preferences of military organizations and civilian leaders. These variations explain the deviations in policy outcomes.

## POLICY IMPLICATIONS: U.S. INSTITUTIONAL STRUCTURE AND INTERNATIONAL CHANGE

A major element in the post–World War II security structure has now changed. Without the Soviet threat, the Army, especially, no longer has the same reason to prepare for a European war. And with the breakup of Eastern Europe, war in Europe no longer looks like the sort of war the U.S. Army wants to fight (as recent developments in Bosnia have demonstrated). Will the Army be more flexible in the post–Cold War era?

> The sad fact is that, with regards to small wars as well as other matters, American civil-military relations is in a state of profound but hidden crisis. Even as portions of the elite (the "military reforms" group, for example, but substantial numbers of both liberals and conservatives) have lost operational confidence in the military, the military has developed an acute mistrust of its civilian masters. The military leadership

in particular has developed a set of requirements for public support unlikely to be met save in the context of a European war; it has convinced itself that it fought the Vietnam War with "a hand tied behind its back," although the amount of human and material forces poured into the war belies that notion.[19]

Given the U.S. Army's bias and the institutional structure in the United States, which makes crisis intervention difficult, policymakers should think twice before trying to change the Army in a hurry and three times before committing Army forces to a situation for which they may be unprepared with the expectation that they will innovate in the field. Short of high levels of cooperation and agreement between Congress and the president, such innovation is unlikely to occur. However, policymakers do affect the Army's bias (as well as the bias of other military organizations) through routine oversight, policy proclamations, and electoral interests. Thus, the Army's bias is not written in stone. It can be changed through cues (intentional or not) from policymakers.

As we have seen throughout discussion of the U.S. case in this book, congressional budgetary decisions have a large effect on the Army's behavior. The effect, however, is neither easy to anticipate nor always what Congress intends. Certainly, budgetary decisions will continue to play a large role in Army behavior, especially in what looks to be a major post–Cold War reduction in forces. The exact effect, however, will depend on how the budgetary issues interact with other issues.

Congressional control over the military has become much more sophisticated in the post–Vietnam period. Congress no longer relies solely on military dissent as analysts of the 1960s argued. Congress has moved both to circumvent presidential power in military matters with the War Powers Act and, more recently, to reorganize the military itself with the Goldwater/Nichols Act.[20] Congressional experts on military and foreign affairs head important committees with large staffs capable of forming their own opinions about military matters.[21]

The degree of congressional expertise on military matters in-

[19] Cohen (1986), p. 295.
[20] For a preliminary assessment of the effects of this act, see Davis (1991).
[21] Blechman (1990).

creases the chances that Congress will act independently of the president on military policy. This may decrease the ability of civilians to force change on the Army. To the degree, however, that it increases Congress's ability to direct military organizations without large inputs from either the president or military organizations,[22] we may see Congress leading the way toward change in the post–Cold War Army. How we view the policy-making process in Congress affects whether we think this is a positive development.[23]

Institutional theory points us toward a systematic comparison of the way structure and process work to prompt policy outcomes. Already, this has generated a wide body of literature comparing domestic policy environments in different countries.[24] This book joins a few others to suggest that a similar approach can be equally important for examining foreign policy and its implications for international relations.[25] The effects of institutions on the growth of military organizations that this book has suggested beg to be tested in other industrial democracies, in the burgeoning number of fledgling democracies, and in nondemocratic settings.

[22] Congressional confidence in its ability to monitor the military free from advice may have been behind its willingness to minimize interservice rivalry with the Goldwater/Nichols Act.

[23] See Mayer (1991) for a defense of Congress in defense contracting. Blechman (1990) also makes the case that Congress is more responsible than not in its conduct of defense policy making. Fiorina (1989) is the classic critique of congressional policy making.

[24] Ames (1987), Bates (1981), Cox (1987), Geddes (1991), North (1981, 1990), Roeder (1993), Shirk (1993).

[25] Cowhey (1990, 1993), Martin (1992), Morrow (1993), O'Halloran (1990), Spruyt (1991).

# Bibliography

## ARCHIVAL SOURCES

CBS/Westmoreland Collection, MSS109. Mandeville Department of Special Collections, University of California, San Diego.

United States Army Military History Institute Archives, Carlisle, Pennsylvania; Personal Papers of William E. Depuy, General Julian J. Ewell, Paul D. Harkins, Harold K. Johnson, George C. Morton, General William B. Rosson, John P. Vann, Volney F. Warner, and Samuel T. Williams.

United States Army Military History Institute Library, Carlisle, Pennsylvania; Officer Debriefing Interviews of Colonel John P. Connor, Brigadier General William R. Desobry, George W. Dickerson, Major-General Charles Duke, George S. Eckhardt, General Julian J. Ewell, and Major-General George I. Forsythe.

## OTHER SOURCES

Adams, Samuel. 1975. "Playing with Numbers." *Harpers,* Jan.–June, p. 250.

Adler, Renata. 1986a. "Annals of Law: Two Trials—I." *New Yorker,* June 16.

Adler, Renata. 1986b. *Reckless Disregard.* New York: Knopf.

Adye, John. 1896. "Has Our Army Grown with Our Empire?" *The Nineteenth Century* 232 (June).

Akerlof, George. 1984. "The Economic Consequences of Cognitive Dissonance." In his *Economic Theorist's Book of Tales.* Cambridge: Cambridge University Press.

Alchian, Armen, and Harold Demsetz. 1972. "Production, Information Costs, and Economic Organization." *American Economic Review* 62.

Aldrich, M. Almy. 1875. *History of the U.S. Marine Corps.* Boston: Shepard.

Alexandroff, Alan, and Richard Rosecrance. 1977. "Deterrence in 1939." *World Politics* 29:3.

Alger, John I. 1982. *The Quest for Victory: The History of the Principles of War.* Westport, Conn.: Greenwood.

Alger, John I. 1985. *Definitions and Doctrine of the Military Art.* Wayne, N.J.: Avery.

# Bibliography

Allison, Graham. 1971. *Essence of Decision: Explaining the Cuban Missile Crisis.* Boston: Little, Brown.

Altfeld, Michael, and Gary Miller. 1984. "Sources of Bureaucratic Influence: Expertise and Agenda Control." *Journal of Conflict Resolution* 28:4.

Ambrose, Stephen E. 1964. *Upton and the Army.* Baton Rouge: Louisiana State University Press.

Ames, Barry. 1987. *Political Survival in Latin America.* Berkeley: University of California Press.

Appy, Christian. 1985. "A War for Nothing: Attitudes of American Soldiers in Vietnam." Harvard University. Typescript.

Art, Robert. 1985. "Bureaucratic Politics and American Foreign Policy: A Critique." In *International Politics: Anarchy, Force, Political Economy, and Decision Making,* ed. Robert J. Art and Robert Jervis. Boston: Little, Brown.

Art, Robert, and Stephen Ockenden. 1981. "The Domestic Politics of Cruise Missile Development, 1970–1980." In *Cruise Missiles: Technology, Strategy, Politics,* ed. Richard Betts. Washington: Brookings Institution.

Art, Robert, and Kenneth Waltz, eds. 1983. *The Use of Force: International Politics and Foreign Policy.* Lanham, Md.: University Press of America.

Bailes, Howard. 1981. "Patterns of Thought in the Late Victorian Army." *Journal of Strategic Studies* 4:1.

Bailey, F. G. 1991. "Why Is Information Asymetrical? Symbolic Behavior in Formal Organizations." University of California, San Diego. Typescript.

Balfour, Michael. 1985. *Britain and Joseph Chamberlain.* London: Allen & Unwin.

Barnett, Corelli. 1970. *Britain and Her Army, 1509–1970.* New York: Morrow.

Bates, Robert. 1981. *Markets and States in Tropical Africa.* Berkeley: University of California Press.

Beckett, Ian, and John Gooch. 1981. *Politicians and Defense: Studies in the Formation of British Defense Policy, 1845– 1970.* Manchester: Manchester University Press.

Beckett, Ian F. W., and Keith Simpson. 1985. *A Nation in Arms.* Manchester: Manchester University Press.

Bendor, Jonathan. 1988. "Review Article: Formal Models of Bureaucracy." *British Journal of Political Science* 18:3.

Bendor, Jonathan, Serge Taylor, and Roland van Gaalen. 1987. "Stacking the Deck: Bureaucratic Missions and Policy Design." *American Political Science Review* 81:3.

Berman, Larry. 1982. *Planning a Tragedy: The Americanization of the War in Vietnam.* New York: Norton.

Bernardo, C. Joseph, and Eugene H. Bacon. 1955. *American Military Policy: Its Development since 1775.* Harrisburg, Pa.: Stackpole.

Best, Geoffrey, and Andrew Wheatcroft, eds. 1976. *War, Economy, and the Military Mind.* London: Croom Helm.

Betts, Richard. 1977. *Soldiers, Statesmen, and the Cold War Crises.* Cambridge: Harvard University Press.

Biddulph, General Sir Robert. 1904. *Lord Cardwell at the War Office.* London: John Murray.

Bidwell, Shelford, and Dominick Graham. 1982. *Firepower: British Army Weapons and Theories of War, 1904–1945.* London: Allen & Unwin.

Binkin, Martin. 1974. *U.S. Reserve Forces: A Problem of the Weekend Warrior.* Washington, D.C.: The Brookings Institution.

Blaufarb, Douglas S. 1977. *The Counterinsurgency Era: U.S. Doctrine and Performance, 1950 to the Present.* New York: Free Press.

Blechman, Barry M. 1990. *The Politics of National Security: Congress and U.S. Defense Policy.* New York: Oxford University Press.

Bond, Brian. 1960. "The Effect of the Cardwell Reforms in Army Organization, 1874–1904." *Journal of the Royal United Services Institution* 105.

Bond, Brian. 1961. "Prelude to the Cardwell Reforms, 1856–68." *Journal of the Royal United Service Institution* 106.

Bond, Brian. 1966. "Doctrine and Training in the British Cavalry." In *The Theory and Practice of War,* ed. Michael Howard. New York: Praeger.

Bond, Brian. 1972. *The Victorian Army and the Staff College.* London: Eyre Methuen.

Bond, Brian. 1980. *British Military Policy Between the Two World Wars.* Oxford: Clarendon Press.

Borklund, C. W. 1968. *The Department of Defense.* New York: Praeger.

Bourne, Kenneth. 1970. *The Foreign Policy of Victorian England, 1830–1902.* Oxford: Clarendon Press.

Bowden, James A. 1982. "The RDJTF and Doctrine." *Military Review* 62:11.

Brehm, John, and Scott Gates. 1990. *Supervision and Control.* Paper presented at the annual meeting of the American Political Science Association, San Francisco.

Brehm, John, and Scott Gates. 1993. "Donut Shops and Speed Traps: Evaluating Models of Supervision on Police Behavior." *American Journal of Political Science* 37:2.

Brodie, Bernard. 1973. *War and Politics.* New York: Macmillan.

Bundy, Harvey H., and others. 1949. "The Organization of the Government for the Conduct of Foreign Affairs." Appendix H. to the *Report of the Commission on Organization of the Executive Branch of the Government.* Washington, February.

Callwell, Colonel C. E. 1976. *Small Wars.* London: EP Publishing.

Calvert, Randall, Mark Moran, and Barry Weingast. 1987. "Congressional Influence over Policymaking: The Case of the FTC." In *Theories of Congress: The New Institutionalism,* ed. Mathew McCubbins and Terry Sullivan. Cambridge: Cambridge University Press.

Cannadine, David. 1990. *The Decline and Fall of the British Aristocracy.* New Haven: Yale University Press.

Caputo, Philip. 1977. *A Rumor of War.* New York: Ballantine Books.

Clark, G. S. 1900. "The Defense of the Empire and the Militia Ballot." *The Nineteenth Century* 275 (Jan.)

Clark, J. C. D. 1985. *English Society, 1688–1832.* Cambridge: Cambridge University Press.

Clutterbuck, Richard L. 1966. *Long, Long, War: Counterinsurgency in Malaya and Vietnam.* New York: Praeger.

Coase, Ronald. 1937. "The Nature of the Firm." *Economica* 4.

Cohen, Eliot. 1985. *Citizens and Soldiers.* Ithaca: Cornell University Press.

Cohen, Eliot. 1986. "Constraints on America's Conduct of Small Wars." In *Conventional Forces and American Defense Policy,* ed. Steven E. Miller. Princeton: Princeton University Press.

Cole, Major D. H., and Major E. C. Priestley. 1936. *An Outline of British Military History, 1660–1936.* London: Sifton, Praed.

Cook, B. J. 1989. "Principal-Agent Models of Political Control of the Bureaucracy." *American Political Science Review* 83:3.

Cowhey, Peter F. 1990. "'States' and 'Politics' in American Foreign Economic Policy." In *International Trade Policies: Gains from Economics and Political Science,* ed. John Odell and Tom Willet. Ann Arbor: University of Michigan Press.

Cowhey, Peter F. 1993. "Domestic Institutions and International Commitments." *International Organization* 47:2.

Cox, Gary. 1987. *The Efficient Secret: The Cabinet and the Development of Political Parties in Victorian England.* New York: Cambridge University Press.

Cox, Gary. 1990. "The Development of Collective Responsibility in the U.K." University of California, San Diego. Typescript.

Cox, Henry B. 1984. *War, Foreign Affairs, and Constitutional Power: 1829–1901.* Cambridge, Mass.: Ballinger.

Craig, Gordon, and Alexander George. 1983. *Force and Statecraft.* New York: Oxford University Press.

Cramer, C. H. 1961. *Newton D. Baker.* New York: World.

Cunliffe, Marcus. 1973. *Soldiers and Civilians: The Martial Spirit in America, 1775–1865.* New York: Free Press.

Davis, Vincent. 1991. "Defense Reorganization and National Security." *Annals of the American Academy of Political Science,* September.

Dawkins, Peter. 1979. "The U.S. Army and the 'Other' War in Vietnam." Ph.D. diss., Princeton University.

Dawson, Raymond. 1963. "Innovation and Intervention in Defense Policy." In *New Perspectives on the House of Representatives,* ed. Robert Peabody and Nelson Polsby. Chicago: Rand McNally.

de Bolch, Jean. 1979. "The Boer War and British Military Theory, 1900–1914." *Journal of Modern History* 51:2.

Derthick, Martha. 1965. *The National Guard in Politics.* Cambridge: Harvard University Press.

Destler, I. M. 1985. "National Security Advice to U.S. Presidents: Some Lessons from Thirty Years." In *U.S. National Security: A Framework for Analysis,* ed. Daniel Kaufman, Jeffrey S. McKitrick, and Thomas J. Leney. Lexington: Lexington Books, D.C. Heath.

Dewar, Michael. 1984. *Brush Fire Wars: Minor Campaigns of the British Army since 1945.* New York: St. Martin's.

DeWitt, David. 1903. *The Impeachment and Trial of Andrew Johnson.* New York: Macmillan.

Dexter, Lewis Anthony. 1969. "Congressmen and the Making of Military Policy." In *New Perspectives on the House of Representatives,* ed. Robert Peabody and Nelson Polsby. Chicago: Rand McNally.

Divine, Robert. 1974. *Foreign Policy and U.S. Presidential Elections.* New York: New Viewpoints.

Downs, Anthony. 1967. *Inside Bureaucracy.* Boston: Little, Brown.

Dupuy, R. E., and T. N. Dupuy. 1970. *The Encyclopedia of Military History, from 3500 B.C. to the Present.* New York: Harper and Row.

Durverger, Maurice. 1950. *Political Parties: Their Organization and Activity in the Modern State.* Trans. Barbara North and Robert North. London: Methuen.

Durverger, Maurice. 1984. "Which Is the Best Electoral System?" In *Choosing an Electoral System,* ed. Arend Lijphart and Bernard Grofman. New York: Praeger.

Earle, Edward M., ed. 1971. *The Makers of Modern Strategy.* Princeton: Princeton University Press.

Elliot, Jonathan. 1854. *Debates on the Federal Constitution.* 4 vols. Washington: Maury and Taylor.

Elsberg, Daniel. 1971. "The Quagmire Myth and the Stalemate Machine." *Public Policy* 19:2.

Emerson, William. 1958. "Franklin Roosevelt as Commander in Chief in WWII." *Military Affairs* 23 (Winter).

Ensor, R. C. K. 1936. *England, 1970–1914.* Oxford: Clarendon.

Fenno, Richard. 1978. *Home Styles: House Members in Their Districts.* Boston: Little, Brown.

Fergusson, Thomas G. 1984. *British Military Intelligence, 1870–1914.* Frederick, Md.: University Publications of America.

Fiorina, Morris P. 1981. "Congressional Control over the Bureaucracy: A Mismatch of Incentives and Capabilities." In *Congress Reconsidered,* ed. Lawrence Dodd and Bruce Oppenheimer. 2d ed. Washington: Congressional Quarterly.

Fiorina, Morris P. 1982. "Legislative Choice of Regulatory Forms: Legal Process or Administrative Process." *Public Choice* 39.

Fiorina, Morris P. 1989. *Congress: Keystone of the Washington Establishment.* New Haven: Yale University Press.

Firth, C. H. 1912. *Cromwell's Army.* London: Methuen.

Flournoy, Francis Rosebro. 1927. *Parliament and War.* London: P. S. King.

Fortescue, J. W. [1910] 1930. *A History of the British Army.* London: Macmillan.

Franck, Thomas M., and Edward Weisband. 1979. *Foreign Policy by Congress.* New York: Oxford University Press.

French, David. 1986. *British Strategy and War Aims, 1915–1916.* London: Allen & Unwin.

Friedberg, Aaron L. 1988. *The Weary Titan: Britain and the Experience of Relative Decline, 1895–1905.* Princeton: Princeton University Press.

Frye, Alton. 1975. *A Responsible Congress: The Politics of National Security.* New York: McGraw-Hill.

Gaddis, John Lewis. 1987. *The Long Peace: Inquiries into the History of the Cold War.* Oxford: Oxford University Press.

Galloway, George B. 1976. *History of the House of Representatives.* New York: Crowell.

Ganoe, William. 1936. *History of the United States Army.* New York: Appleton-Century.

Gash, N. 1965. *Reaction and Reconstruction in English Politics, 1832–1852.* London: Clarendon Press.

Gaubatz, Kurt Taylor. 1990. "Pro-War Publics, Anti-War Elites." Paper presented at the annual meeting of the American Political Science Association, San Francisco.

Geddes, Barbara. 1991. "A Game Theoretical Model of Reform in Latin American Democracies." *American Political Science Review* 85:2.

Gelb, Leslie, and Richard Betts. 1979. *The Irony of Vietnam: The System Worked.* Washington: Brookings Institution.

Glover, Richard. 1963. *Peninsular Preparation: The Reform of the British Army, 1795–1809.* London. Cambridge University Press.

Goldman, Charles Sydney. 1902. *With General French and the Cavalry in South Africa.* London: Macmillan.

Goldstein, Judith. 1989. "The Impact of Ideas on Trade Policy: The Origins of U.S. Agricultural and Manufacturing Policies." *International Organization* 43:1.

Gooch, John. 1974. *The Plans of War: The General Staff and British Military Strategy, c. 1900–1916.* London: Routledge & Kegan Paul.

Gooch, John. 1981. *The Prospect of War.* London: Cass.

Gordon, Michael R. 1974. "Domestic Conflict and the Origins of the First World War." *Journal of Modern History* 46.

Gourevitch, Peter. 1978. "Second Image Reversed: The International Sources of Domestic Politics." *International Organization* 32:3–4.

*Bibliography*

Grant, Steven. 1990. "Small War and Regular War." Paper presented at the annual meeting of the American Political Science Association, San Francisco.

Greenfield, K. R. 1963. *American Strategy in WWII: A Reconsideration.* Baltimore: Johns Hopkins University Press.

Grofman, Bernard, and Arend Lijphart, eds. 1986. *Electoral Laws and Their Political Consequences.* New York: Agathon.

Gronich, Lori Helene. 1989. "The Cognitive Processing Theory of Decision Making: A New Explanation for Policies of War and Peace." Paper presented at the annual meeting of the American Political Science Association.

Guest, H. M. 1902. *With Lord Methuen and the First Division.* Klersdorp, Transvaal: H. M. Guest.

Haggard, Stephan. 1988. "The Institutional Foundations of Hegemony: Explaining the Reciprocal Trade Agreements Act of 1934." In *The State and American Foreign Policy,* ed. G. John Ikenberry. Ithaca: Cornell University Press.

Hale, Maj. Lansdale. 1876. "The Study of Military History by the Regimental Officers of the Army." *Journal of the Royal United Service Institution* 20.

Halperin, Morton H. 1974. *Bureaucratic Politics and Foreign Policy.* Washington, D.C.: Brookings.

Hamer, W. S. 1970. *The British Army: Civil-Military Relations, 1885–1905.* Oxford: Clarendon Press.

Hammond, Paul. 1961. *Organizing for Defense.* Princeton: Princeton University Press.

Hammond, Thomas, and Gary Miller. 1985. "A Social Choice Perspective on Expertise and Authority in Bureaucracy." *American Journal of Political Science* 29:1.

Haswell, Jock. 1975. *The British Army.* London: Thames and Hudson.

Heinl, Colonel Robert D. 1962. *Soldiers of the Sea.* Annapolis: U.S. Naval Institute.

Henderson, G. F. R. 1905. *The Science of War.* London: Longmans, Green.

Herring, George. 1986. *America's Longest War: The United States and Vietnam, 1950–1975.* New York: Alfred A. Knopf.

Hilsman, Roger. 1967. *To Move a Nation.* Garden City, N.Y.: Doubleday.

Hirshman, Albert. 1970. *Exit, Voice, and Loyalty: Responses to Decline in Firms, Organizations, and States.* Cambridge: Harvard University Press.

Hobson, John A., and George P. Gooch. 1972. *The War in South Africa: Its Causes and Effects.* New York: Garland.

Horton, Frank B., ed. 1974. *Comparative Defense Policy.* Baltimore: Johns Hopkins University Press.

Howard, Michael. 1965. *The Theory and Practice of War.* New York: Praeger.

Howarth, David. 1974. *Sovereign of the Seas.* New York: Athenaeum.

Huntington, Samuel. 1957. *The Soldier and the State.* Cambridge: Harvard University Press.

Huntington, Samuel. 1965. "The Interim Years: World War II to January, 1950." In *American Defense Policy in Perspective,* ed. Raymond G. O'Connor. New York: John Wiley & Sons.

Huntington, Samuel. 1968. *Political Order in Changing Societies.* New Haven: Yale University Press.

Huntington, Samuel. 1982. *The Strategic Imperative: New Politics for American Security.* Cambridge, Mass.: Ballinger.

Hyman, Harold M. 1960. "Johnson, Stanton, and Grant." *American Historical Review* 65.

Isely, Jeter A., and Philip A. Crowl. 1951. *U.S. Marines and Amphibious War.* Princeton: Princeton University Press.

Jacobs, James Ripley. 1947. *The Beginning of the U.S. Army*. Princeton: Princeton University Press.

Jacobson, Gary. 1983. *The Politics of Congressional Elections*. Boston: Little, Brown.

Janowitz, Morris. 1960. *The Professional Soldier: A Social and Political Portrait*. New York: Free Press.

Jervis, Robert. 1976. *Perception and Misperception in International Politics*. Princeton: Princeton University Press.

Jervis, Robert. 1978. "Cooperation under the Security Dilemma." *World Politics* 30:2.

Johnson, Franklyn Arthur. 1960. *Defense by Committee: The British Committee of the Imperial Defense, 1885–1959*. London: Oxford University Press.

Johnson, Loch K. 1988. *A Season of Inquiry: Congress and Intelligence*. Chicago: Dorsey.

Johnson, Loch K. 1989a. "Covert Action and Accountability: Decision-Making for America's Secret Foreign Policy." *International Studies Quarterly* 33.

Johnson, Loch K. 1989b. *America's Secret Power: The CIA in a Democratic Society*. New York: Oxford University Press.

Johnston, Michael. 1993. "Historical Conflict and the Rise of Standards." In *The Global Resurgence of Democracy*, ed. Larry Diamond. Baltimore: Johns Hopkins University Press.

Kaiser, David E. 1980. "Vietnam: Was the System the Solution?" *International Security* 4:4.

Keegan, John. 1976. *The Face of Battle*. New York: Viking.

Keiser, Gordon W. 1982. *U.S. Marine Corps and Defense Unification, 1944–1947*. Washington: National Defense University Press.

Kelly, Colonel Francis J. 1973. *U.S Army Special Forces, 1961–1971*. Washington: Department of the Army.

Kendrick, M. Slade. 1955. *A Century and a Half of Federal Expenditures*. National Bureau of Economic Research, Occasional Paper 48.

Kennedy, Paul M., ed. 1979. *War Plans of the Great Powers*. London: Allen and Unwin.

Kennedy, Paul. 1987. *The Rise and Fall of the Great Powers*. New York: Vintage.

Kernell, Samuel. 1977. "Toward Understanding Nineteenth Century Congressional Careers." *American Journal of Political Science* 21:4.

Kier, Elizabeth. 1992. "Changes in Conventional Military Doctrines: The Cultural Roots of Doctrinal Change." Ph.D. diss., Cornell University.

Kiewiet, D. Roderick, and Mathew McCubbins. 1991. *The Logic of Delegation: Congressional Parties and the Appropriation Process*. Chicago: University of Chicago Press.

Knightly, Phillip. 1978. *The First Casualty*. London: Quartet.

Knott, Jack, and Gary Miller. 1987. *Reforming Bureaucracy: The Politics of Institutional Choice*. Englewood Cliffs, N.J.: Prentice-Hall.

Koh, Harold Hongju. 1990. *The National Security Constitution: Sharing Power after the Iran-Contra Affair*. New Haven: Yale University Press.

Kolodziej, Edward A. 1966. *The Uncommon Defense and Congress, 1945–1963*. Columbus: Ohio State University Press.

Komer, Robert. 1972. *The Malayan Emergency in Retrospect: Organization of a Successful Counterinsurgency Effort*. Santa Monica: Rand.

Komer, Robert. 1986. *Bureaucracy at War: U.S. Performance in the Vietnam Conflict*. Boulder, Colo.: Westview.

Krasner, Stephen. 1972. "Are Bureaucracies Important? or, Allison Wonderland." *Foreign Policy* 7.

Kreidberg, Marvin A., and Merton G. Henry. 1955. *History of Military Mobilization in the United States Army, 1775–1945*. Washington: Department of the Army.

Bibliography

Krepinevich, Andrew F., Jr. 1986. *The Army in Vietnam*. Baltimore: Johns Hopkins University Press.

Kreps, Donald. 1990. "Corporate Culture and Economic Theory." In *Perspectives on Positive Political Economy*, ed. James Alt and Kenneth Shepsle. New York: Cambridge University Press.

Krulak, Victor H. 1984. *First to Fight: An Inside View of the U.S. Marine Corps*. Annapolis: U.S. Naval Institute.

Leary, William M., ed. 1984. *The Central Intelligence Agency: History and Documents*. University: University of Alabama Press.

Liddell Hart, B. H. 1939. *The Defense of Britain*. New York: Random House.

Lijphart, Arend. 1984. *Democracies: Patterns of Majoritarian and Consensus Government in Twenty-One Countries*. New Haven: Yale University Press.

Lincoln, Abraham. 1953–55. *The Collected Works of Abraham Lincoln*, ed. Roy P. Basler. 9 vols. New Brunswick: Rutgers University Press.

Linz, Juan J., and Arturo Valenzuala, eds. 1992. *Presidential or Parliamentary Democracy: Does It Make a Difference?* Baltimore: Johns Hopkins University Press.

Luttwak, Edward. 1981. "The Operational Level of War." *International Security* 5:3.

Luttwak, Edward N. 1983. "Notes on Low Intensity Warfare." *Parameters* 13:4.

Luttwak, Edward. 1985. *The Pentagon and the Art of War*. New York: Simon & Schuster.

Luvaas, Jay. 1964. *The Education of an Army: British Military Thought, 1815–1940*. Chicago: University of Chicago Press.

McCormick, Richard L. 1986. *The Party Period and Public Policy*. New York: Oxford University Press.

McCubbins, Mathew, and Thomas Schwartz. 1984. "Congressional Oversight Overlooked: Police Patrols versus Fire Alarms." *American Journal of Political Science* 28:1.

McCubbins, Mathew D. 1985. "The Legislative Design of Regulatory Structure." *American Journal of Political Science* 29:4.

McCubbins, Mathew D. 1983. "Policy Components of Arms Competition." *American Journal of Political Science*, 27:3.

McCubbins, Mathew, and Terry Sullivan, eds. 1987. *Congress: Structure and Policy*. Cambridge: Cambridge University Press.

McDermott, J. 1979. "The Revolution in British Military Thinking from the Boer War to the Moroccan Crisis." In *The War Plans of the Great Powers, 1880–1914*, ed. Paul Kennedy. London: Allen & Unwin.

McGarvey, Patrick. 1970. "D.I.A.: Intelligence to Please." *Washington Monthly* 2:1 – 6.

Mack, Andrew J. R. 1983. "Why Big Countries Lose Small Wars: The Politics of Asymetric Conflict." In *Power, Strategy, and Security: A World Politics Reader*, ed. Klaus Knoff. Princeton: Princeton University Press.

McNaughter, Thomas. 1989. "Weapons Procurement: The Futility of Reform." In *America's Defenses*, ed. Michael Mandelbaum. New York: Holmes & Meier.

Mangold, Tom, and John Penycate. 1986. *The Tunnels of Cu Chi*. New York: Berkley Books.

March, James, and Johan Olsen. 1984. "The New Institutionalism." *American Political Science Review* 78:3.

March, James, and Herbert Simon. 1958. *Organizations*. New York: John Wiley and Sons.

Marr, David. 1971. "The Rise and Fall of Counterinsurgency." In *The Pentagon Papers*, Senator Gravel Edition, vol. 5. Boston: Beacon.

Martin Lisa. 1992. "Legislative Delegation and International Engagement." Paper

[149]

presented at the annual meeting of the American Political Science Association, Chicago.

Matloff, Maurice. 1959. *Strategic Planning for Coalitional Warfare, 1943–1944.* Washington: Department of the Army.

Matloff, Maurice. 1965. "The American Approach to War, 1919–1945." In *The Theory and Practice of War,* ed. Michael Howard. New York: Praeger.

Maude, F. N. 1907. *War and the World's Life.* London: Smith, Elder.

Maude, F. N. 1908. *The Leipzig Campaign.* London: Sonnenschein.

Maurice, John Frederick. 1906–1910. *History of the War in South Africa.* London: Hurst & Blackett.

Mayer, Kenneth R. 1991. *The Political Economy of Defense Contracting.* New Haven: Yale University Press.

Mayhew, David. 1974. *Congress: The Electoral Connection.* New Haven: Yale University Press.

Means, George P. 1976. *Malaysian Politics.* London: Hodder & Stoughton.

Mearsheimer, John. 1983. *Conventional Deterrence.* Ithaca: Cornell University Press.

Metcalf, Colonel Clyde. 1939. *History of the Marine Corps.* New York: Putnam's Sons.

Miller, Gary. 1992. *Managerial Dilemmas: The Political Economy of Hierarchy.* Cambridge: Cambridge University Press.

Miller, Gary J., and Terry M. Moe. 1986. "The Positive Theory of Hierarchies." In *Political Science: The Study of Politics,* ed. Herbert Weisberg. New York: Agathon.

Miller, Harry. 1954. *Menace in Malaya.* London: Harrap.

Miller, Stephen, ed. 1985. *Military Strategy and the Origins of the First World War.* Princeton: Princeton University Press.

Millett, Alan R. 1980. *Semper Fidelis: The History of the United States Marine Corps.* New York: Macmillan.

Millis, Walter, Harvey Mansfield, and Harold Stein. 1958. *Arms and the State.* New York: Twentieth Century Fund.

Milne, R. S., and D. Mauzy. 1977. *Politics and Government in Malaysia.* Singapore: Federal Publications.

Moe, Terry. 1984. "The New Economics of Organization." *American Journal of Political Science* 28:4.

Moe, Terry. 1985. "The Politicized Presidency." In *The New Direction in American Politics,* ed. Paul Peterson and John Chubb. Washington: Brookings Institution.

Moe, Terry. 1987. "An Assessment of the Positive Theory of 'Congressional Dominance'." *Legislative Studies Quarterly* 12:4.

Moe, Terry. 1990. "The Politics of Structural Choice: Toward a Theory of Public Bureaucracy." In *Organizational Theory: From Chester Barnard to the Present and Beyond,* ed. Oliver Williamson. New York: Oxford University Press.

Morgenthau, Hans. 1978. *Politics among Nations.* New York: Knopf.

Morrow, James. 1993. "Arms versus Allies: Trade-Offs in the Search for Security." *International Organization* 47:2.

Moskos, Charles. 1970. *The American Enlisted Man.* New York: Russell Sage Foundation.

Nelson, Anna Kasten. 1981. "National Security I: Inventing a Process." In *The Illusion of Presidential Government,* ed. Hugh Heclo and Lester M. Soloman. Boulder, Colo.: Westview.

Neustadt, Richard. [1960] 1980. *Presidential Power: The Politics of Leadership from FDR to Carter.* New York: Wiley & Sons.

North, Douglas. 1981. *Structure and Change in Economic History*. New York: Norton.

North, Douglas. 1990. *Institutions, Institutional Change, and Economic Performance*. New York: Cambridge University Press.

O'Ballance, Edgar. 1966. *Malaya: The Communist Insurgent War, 1948–1960*. Hamden, Conn.: Archon.

Odell, John. 1982. *U.S. International Monetary Policy*. Princeton: Princeton University Press.

O'Gorman, Frank. 1982. *The Emergence of the British Two Party System*. New York: Holmes and Meier.

O'Halloran, Sharon. 1990. "Congress, the President, and U.S. Trade Policy: Process and Policy Outcome." Paper presented at the annual meeting of the American Political Science Association, San Francisco.

Olson, Mancur. 1965. *The Logic of Collective Action*. Cambridge: Harvard University Press.

Omond, J. S. 1933. *Parliament and the Army, 1642–1904*. Cambridge: Cambridge University Press.

Otley, C. B. 1968. "Militarism and the Social Affiliations of the British Army Elite." In *Armed Forces and Society*, ed. Jacques Van Doorne. The Hague: Mouton.

Packenham, Thomas. 1979. *The Boer War*. New York: Random House.

Palmer, Bruce. 1984. *The Twenty-Five Year War: America's Military Role in Vietnam*. Lexington: University Press of Kentucky.

Palmer, Gregory. 1978. *The McNamara Strategy and the Vietnam War*. Westport, Conn.: Greenwood.

Paxon, Frederic L. 1939. *America at War, 1917–1918*. Boston: Houghton Mifflin.

*The Pentagon Papers: The Defense Department History of United States Decisionmaking on Vietnam*. 1971–72. Senator Gravel Edition. 5 vols. Boston: Beacon.

Perlmutter, Amos. 1977. *The Military and Politics in Modern Times: On Professionals, Praetorians, and Revolutionary Soldiers*. New Haven: Yale University Press.

Peterson, Michael. 1989. *The Combined Action Platoons: The U.S. Marines' Other War in Vietnam*. New York: Praeger.

Pierson, Paul. 1993. "When Effect Becomes Cause: Policy Feedback and Political Change." *World Politics* 45:4.

Pond, Elizabeth. 1972. "South Vietnamese Politics and the American Withdrawal." In *Indochina in Conflict*, ed. Joseph Zasloff and Allen Goodman. Lexington, Mass.: Heath.

Popkin, Samuel. 1979. *The Rational Peasant*. Berkeley: University of California Press.

Popkin, Samuel. 1991. *The Reasoning Voter*. Chicago: University of Chicago Press.

Posen, Barry R. 1984. *The Sources of Military Doctrine: France, Britain, and Germany between the World Wars*. Ithaca: Cornell University Press.

Powell, Walter, and Paul DiMaggio, eds. 1991. *The New Institutionalism in Organizational Analysis*. Chicago: University of Chicago Press.

Price, H. Douglas. 1971. "The Congressional Career: Then and Now." In *Congressional Behavior*, ed. Nelson Polsby. New York: Random House.

Purcell, Victor. 1954. *Malaya: Communist or Free?* London: Gollancz.

Pye, Lucian. 1956. *Guerrilla Communism in Malaya*. Princeton: Princeton University Press.

Race, Jeffrey. 1972. *War Comes to Long An*. Berkeley: University of California Press.

Ranelagh, John. 1986. *The Agency: The Rise and Decline of the CIA*. New York: Simon & Schuster.

Reardon, Carol. 1990. *Soldiers and Scholars: The U.S. Army and the Uses of Military History, 1865–1920.* Lawrence: University Press of Kansas.

Reis, John C. 1964. *The Management of Defense: Organization and Control of the U.S. Armed Services.* Baltimore: Johns Hopkins University Press.

Richmond, Admiral Sir Herbert. 1946. *Statesmen and Sea Power.* Oxford: Clarendon Press.

Riddle, Donald H. 1964. *The Truman Committee.* New Brunswick, N.J.: Rutgers University Press.

Riker, William H. 1979. *Soldiers of the States.* New York: Arno Press.

Riker, William. 1980. "Implications from the Disequilibrium of Majority Rule for the Study of Institutions." *American Political Science Review* 74:2.

Risch, Erna. 1962. *Quartermaster Support for the Army.* Washington: Department of the Army.

Rodenbough, General Theodore F. 1879. "The Militia of the United States." *United Service* (n.s.) 1, April.

Roeder, Philip. 1993. *Red Sunset.* Princeton: Princeton University Press.

Rogers, Lt. Gen. Bernard William. 1974. *Cedar Falls–Junction City: A Turning Point.* Washington: Department of the Army.

Rogowski, Ronald. 1978. "Rationalist Theories of Politics: A Midterm Report." *World Politics* 30:2.

Rogowski, Ronald. 1987. "Trade and the Variety of Domestic Institutions." *International Organization* 41:2.

Rosen, Stephen Peter. 1982. "Vietnam and the American Theory of Limited War." *International Security* 7:2.

Rosen, Stephen Peter. 1988. "New Ways of War: Understanding Military Innovation." *International Security* 13:1.

Rosen, Stephen Peter. 1991. *Winning the Next War: Innovation and the Modern Military.* Ithaca: Cornell University Press.

Ross, Dennis. 1989. "American Military Policy outside Europe." In *America's Defenses,* ed. Michael Mandelbaum. New York: Holmes & Meier.

Rosson, William B. 1962. "Accent on Cold War Capability." *Army Information Digest* 17 (May).

Rosson, William B. 1978. "Four Periods of American Involvement in Vietnam: Development and Implementation of Policy, Strategy, and Programs, Described and Analysed on the Basis of Service Experience at Progressively Senior Levels." Ph.D. diss., Oxford University.

Ruggie, John. 1986. "Continuity and Transformation in the World Polity." In *Neorealism and Its Critics,* ed. Robert Keohane. New York: Columbia University Press.

Rust, William J. 1985. *Kennedy in Vietnam: American Vietnam Policy, 1960–1963.* New York: Charles Scribner's Sons.

Schilling, Warner, Paul Hammond, and Glen Snyder. 1962. *Strategy, Politics, and Defense Budgets.* New York: Columbia University Press.

Scouller, Major R. E. 1966. *The Armies of Queen Anne.* Oxford: Clarendon.

Selby, John. 1969. *The Boer War: A Study of Cowardice and Courage.* London: Arthur Barker.

Selby, John. 1970. "The Boer War." In *History of the British Army,* ed. Peter Young and J. P. Lawford. New York: Putnam.

Shafer, D. Michael. 1988. *Deadly Paradigms: The Failure of U.S. Counterinsurgency Policy.* Princeton: Princeton University Press.

Shapley, Deborah. 1993. *Promise and Power: The Life and Times of Robert McNamara.* Boston: Little, Brown.

Sharp, Admiral U. S. Grant. 1978. *Strategy for Defeat: Vietnam in Retrospect.* San Rafael, Calif.: Presidio.

Shepsle, Kenneth. 1979. "Institutional Arrangements and Equilibrium in Multidimensional Voting Models." *American Journal of Political Science* 23:1.

Shepsle, Kenneth. 1986. "Institutional Equilibrium and Equilibrium Institutions." In *Political Science: The Science of Politics,* ed. Herbert F. Weisberg. New York: Agathon.

Shirk, Susan. 1993. *The Political Logic of Economic Reform in China.* Berkeley: University of California Press.

Shugart, Matthew, and John Carey. 1992. *Presidents and Assemblies: Constitutional Design and Electoral Dynamics.* Cambridge: Cambridge University Press.

Simmons, Brig. Gen. E. H., et al. 1974. *The Marines in Vietnam.* Washington: Department of the Navy.

Skowronek, Stephen. 1982. *Building a New American State.* Cambridge: Cambridge University Press.

Smith, Charles R. 1975. *Marines in the Revolution.* Washington: U.S. Marine Corps History and Museums Division.

Smith, Lewis. 1951. *American Democracy and Military Power.* Chicago: University of Chicago Press.

Smith, Paul. 1919. "The Militia of the United States from 1846 to 1860." *Indiana Magazine of History* 15, March.

Smith, R. B. 1983. *An International History of the Vietnam War.* Vol. II. London: Macmillan.

Smyrl, Marc. 1988. *Conflict or Codetermination: Congress, the President, and the Power to Make War.* Cambridge, Mass.: Ballinger.

Snyder, Jack. 1984. *Ideology of the Offensive: Military Decision Making and the Disasters of 1914.* Ithaca: Cornell University Press.

Snyder, Jack. 1991. *Myths of Empire.* Ithaca: Cornell University Press.

Solt, L. F. 1959. *Saints in Arms: Puritanism and Democracy in Cromwell's Army.* Stanford: Sanford University Press.

Spector, Ronald H. 1983. *U.S. Army in Vietnam.* Vol. 1: *Advice and Support: The Early Years, 1941–1960.* Washington: U.S. Army Center of Military History.

Spies, S. B. 1977. *Methods of Barbarism?* Cape Town: Herman and Rousseau.

Spires, Edward M. 1980. *The Army and Society, 1815–1914.* London: Longman.

Spruyt, Hendrik. 1991. "The Sovereign State and Its Competitors." Ph.D. diss., University of California, San Diego.

Stagg, J.C.A. 1983. *Mr. Madison's War: Politics, Diplomacy, and Warfare in the Early American Republic.* Princeton: Princeton University Press.

Starry, Gen. Donne A. 1978. *Mounted Combat in Vietnam.* Vietnam Studies. Washington: GPO.

Steele, Capt. Matthew Forney. 1909. *American Campaigns.* 2 vols. Washington: Byron S. Adams.

Steinbruner, John. 1974. *The Cybernetic Theory of Decision.* Princeton: Princeton University Press.

Stenson, Michael. 1980. *Class, Race, and Colonialism in West Malaysia.* Vancouver: University of British Columbia Press.

Stephens, Herbert W. 1971. "The Role of the Legislative Committees in the Appropriations Process: A Study Focused on the Armed Services Committee." *Western Political Quarterly* 24.

[153]

Sternberg, Count Adalbert. 1901. *My Experiences of the Boer War*. London: Longmans, Green.

Stone, Jay. 1985. "The Boer War and Its Effects on British Military Reform." Ph.D. diss., City University of New York.

Stone, Jay, and Erwin Schmidl. 1988. *The Boer War and Military Reforms*. Lanham, Md.: University Press of America.

Strachan, Hew. 1984. *The Reform of the British Army, 1830–1854*. Manchester: Manchester University Press.

Strachan, Hew. 1985. *From Waterloo to Balaclava: Tactics, Technology, and the British Army, 1815–1854*. Cambridge: Cambridge University Press.

Stubbs, Richard. 1989. *Hearts and Minds in Guerrilla Warfare: The Malayan Emergency, 1848–1960*. Singapore: Oxford University Press.

Sweetman, John. 1984. *War and Administration*. Edinburgh: Scottish Academic Press.

Symons, Julian. 1963. *Buller's Campaign*. London: Cresset.

Taagepera, Rein, and Matthew Shugart. 1989. *Seats and Votes: The Effects and Determinants of Electoral Systems*. New Haven: Yale University Press.

Thain, Raphial P. 1901. *Legislative History of the General Staff of the United States from 1775 to 1901*. Washington: GPO.

Thayer, Thomas C. 1977. "The American Style of War Made It Costly." In *The Lessons of Vietnam*, ed. W. Scott Thompson and Donald D. Frizzell. New York: Crane, Russak.

Thomas, Benjamin P., and Harold M. Hyman. 1962. *Stanton: The Life and Times of Lincoln's Secretary of War*. New York: Knopf.

Thompson, James D. 1967. *Organizations in Action*. New York: McGraw-Hill.

Thompson, James. 1989. "How Could Vietnam Happen? An Autopsy." In *American Foreign Policy: Theoretical Essays*, ed. G. John Ikenberry. New York: HarperCollins.

Thompson, Brigadier Sir Robert, RA (Ret.). 1969. *No Exit from Vietnam*. New York: McKay.

Thompson, W. Scott, and Donald D. Frizzell, eds. 1977. *The Lessons of Vietnam*. New York: Crane, Russak.

*The Times History of the War in South Africa*. 1900–1909. London: Low, Marston.

Tolson, Lt. Gen. John J. III. 1973. *Airmobility, 1961–1971*. Vietnam Studies. Washington: GPO.

Trachtenberg, Marc. 1991. "The Meaning of Mobilization in 1914." *International Security* 15:3.

Travers, T. H. E. 1979. "Technology, Tactics, and Morale: Jean de Bloch, the Boer War, and British Military Theory, 1900–1914." *Journal of Modern History* 51.

Travers, T. H. E. 1987. *The Killing Ground*. London: Allen & Unwin.

Tsebelis, George. 1990. *Nested Games: Rational Choice in Comparative Politics*. Berkeley: University of California Press.

U.S. Army Command and General Staff College. 1959–61. *Program of Instruction for 250-A-C2 Command and General Staff College Office Regular Course*. Fort Leavenworth, Kans.: C&GSC.

U.S. Army Command and General Staff College. 1963–67. *Program for Command and General Staff Officer Course*. Fort Leavenworth, Kans.: C&GSC.

U.S. Department of Combat Development. 1957. *Estimate of the Situation*. Fort Rucker, Alaska: U.S. Army Aviation School.

U.S. Department of Defense. 1971. *U.S.–Vietnam Relations*. Washington: GPO.

Upton, Emory. 1972. *The Armies of Asia and Europe*. Westport, Conn.: Greenwood.

Upton, Emory. 1904. *The Military Policy in the United States*. Washington, D.C.: Government Printing Office.

USCONARC, Historical Division, 1962. "Special Warfare Board Final Report." In *Summary of Major Events and Problems*, hq, USCONARC.

Van Doorne, Jacques, ed. 1968. *Armed Forces and Society*. The Hague: Mouton.

Van Doorne, Jacques. 1975. *The Soldier and Social Change*. London: Sage.

Van Evera, Stephen. 1985. "Why Cooperation Failed in 1914." *World Politics* 38:1.

Vincent, Sir Howard. 1900. "Lessons of the War: Personal Observations and Impressions of the Forces and Military Establishments Now in South Africa." *Journal of the Royal United Service Institution* 44.

Vorys, K. von. 1976. *Democracy without Consensus*. Singapore: Oxford University Press.

Waltz, Kenneth. 1959. *Man, the State, and War: A Theoretical Analysis*. New York: Columbia University Press.

Waltz, Kenneth. 1979. *Theory of International Politics*. New York: Random House.

Weber, Max. 1964. *The Theory of Social and Economic Organization*. New York: The Free Press.

Weigley, Russell F. 1962. *Toward an American Army: Military Thought from Washington to Marshall*. New York: Columbia University Press.

Weigley, Russell. [1967] 1984. *The History of the United States Army*. Bloomington: Indiana University Press.

Weigley, Russell. 1976. "Military Strategy and Civilian Leadership." In *Historical Dimensions of National Security Problems*, ed. Klaus Knorr. Lawrence: University of Kansas Press.

Weingast, Barry. 1979. "A Rational Choice Perspective on Congressional Norms." *American Journal of Political Science* 23:2.

Weingast, Barry, and Mark Moran. 1983. "Bureaucratic Discretion or Congressional Control: Regulatory Policymaking by the Federal Trade Commission." *Journal of Political Economy* 91:5.

Weingast, Barry, Kenneth Shepsle, and Christopher Johnson. 1981. "The Political Economy of Benefits and Costs: A Neoclassical Approach to Distributive Politics." *Journal of Political Economy* 89:4.

West, F. J. 1985. *The Village*. Madison: University of Wisconsin Press.

Wheeler, Earle. N.d. *Addresses by General Earle Wheeler, Chairman, Joint Chiefs of Staff*. 2 vols. N.p.

White, Leonard D. 1958. *The Republican Era, 1869–1901: A Study in Administrative History*. New York: Macmillan.

Williams, T. Harry. 1952. *Lincoln and His Generals*. New York: Knopf.

Wilson, James Q. 1989. *Bureaucracy: What Government Agencies Do and Why They Do It*. New York: Basic Books.

Winton, Harold. 1988. *To Change an Army*. Lawrence: University of Kansas Press.

Wirtz, James J. 1988. "Explaining an Instance of Intrawar Intelligence Failure: The American Military's Response to the 1968 TET Offensive." Ph.D. diss., Columbia University.

Wirtz, James J. 1990. "Intelligence to Please? The Order of Battle Controversy during the Vietnam War." Department of National Security Affairs, Naval Postgraduate School, Monterey, Calif. Typescript.

Wolfers, Arnold. 1956. *The Anglo-American Tradition in Foreign Affairs*. New Haven: Yale University Press.

Wolfers, Arnold. 1963. *Britain and France between Two Wars*. Hamden, Conn.: Archon.

Wood, B. D. 1988. "Principals, Bureaucrats, and Responsiveness in Clean Air Enforcements." *American Political Science Review* 82:1.

Woodward, E. L. 1964. *Great Britain and the German Navy.* Hamden, Conn.: Archon.

Zisk, K. M. 1990. "Soviet Reactions to Shifts in U.S. and NATO Military Doctrine in Europe: The Defense Policy Community and Innovation." Ph.D. diss., Stanford University.

# *Index*

Adams, Samuel, 93
Adler, Renata, 94
adverse selection, 6
agency loss, 6–7, 103, 132, 137
  *See also* principal-agent relationship
agenda setting, 6, 35
  lack of, in British Army, 46
  U.S. Army's control over, in Viet-
    nam, 87–94, 100–101
airborne division, of the U.S. Army, 66
Airforce, U.S., 35, 50–51, 67–68, 73, 84
  and special forces air power, 64n48
airmobile division, of the U.S. Army,
  66–69, 75
American Revolution, 37
armored division, British before WWII,
  116, 129
Army of the Republic of Vietnam
  (ARVN), 53, 55, 95–96
Art, Robert, 132n4, 136n10
artillery, British, 109–10
art of war, 28

balance of power theory, 5, 7, 18, 19
Berman, Larry, 70–71
Betts, Richard, 71–72
Black Week, 107
Blanchard, George, 65
Baufarb, Douglas, 73
blockhouses, 113
body count, 91, 99–101
Briggs, Sir Herald, 120, 122, 124
Broderick, St. John, 112
Budget Act of 1921, 50

budgets. *See* civilian oversight tools:
  budgets
Buller, Sir Redvers, 104–6, 108, 110–14

Cardwell, Edward, 37
Cardwell reforms, 38, 41n57
career incentives, 17, 74, 97, 130,
  133–34
  in the British Army, 38–40, 46
  in the CIA, 80–84
  in the U.S. Army, 28, 34–35, 66, 75
  in the U.S. Army Special Forces,
    65–66
  in the U.S. Marines, 84–87
cavalry, British, 105, 109–11
Central Intelligence Agency (CIA), 52
  and creation of counterinsurgency
    doctrine, 76–77, 95, 100
  direction of CIDGs in Vietnam,
    61–63, 78
  failure to control doctrine in Viet-
    nam, 87–88
  institutional development of, 80–84,
    139
  and order of battle controversy, 90,
    92–94
Chamberlain, Joseph, 106–7
Churchill, Winston, 118, 127–28
civilian intervention, 5, 13–15, 19–20,
  74, 130, 133, 135
  in crises, 14, 116–17, 140
  effects on British professionalism,
    40, 46
  lack of, in Britain, 118

## CORNELL STUDIES IN SECURITY AFFAIRS

*edited by* Robert J. Art, Robert Jervis,
*and* Stephen M. Walt

*Political Institutions and Military Change: Lessons from Peripheral Wars,*
by Deborah D. Avant
*Strategic Nuclear Targeting,* edited by Desmond Ball and Jeffrey Richelson
*Japan Prepares for Total War: The Search for Economic Security, 1919–1941,*
by Michael A. Barnhart
*The German Nuclear Dilemma,* by Jeffrey Boutwell
*Flying Blind: The Politics of the U.S. Strategic Bomber Program,*
by Michael L. Brown
*Citizens and Soldiers: The Dilemmas of Military Service,* by Eliot A. Cohen
*Great Power Politics and the Struggle over Austria, 1945–1955,*
by Audrey Kurth Cronin
*Military Organizations, Complex Machines: Modernization in the U.S. Armed
Services,* by Chris C. Demchak
*Nuclear Arguments: Understanding the Strategic Nuclear Arms and Arms Control
Debate,* edited by Lynn Eden and Steven E. Miller
*Public Opinion and National Security in Western Europe,*
by Richard C. Eichenberg
*Innovation and the Arms Race: How the United States and the Soviet Union
Develop New Military Technologies,* by Matthew Evangelista
*Israel's Nuclear Dilemma,* by Yair Evron
*Guarding the Guardians: Civilian Control of Nuclear Weapons in the United
States,* by Peter Douglas Feaver
*Men, Money, and Diplomacy: The Evolution of British Strategic Foreign Policy,
1919–1926,* by John Robert Ferris
*A Substitute for Victory: The Politics of Peacekeeping at the Korean Armistice Talks,*
by Rosemary Foot
*The Wrong War: American Policy and the Dimensions of the Korean Conflict,
1950–1953,* by Rosemary Foot
*The Best Defense: Policy Alternatives for U.S. Nuclear Security from the 1950s to
the 1990s,* by David Goldfischer